PEOPLES OF ROMAN BRITAIN

General Editor Keith Branigan
Lecturer in Archaeology in the University of Bristol

THE
TRINOVANTES

ROSALIND DUNNETT

Formerly Director of Excavations
Colchester Excavation Committee

DUCKWORTH

First published in 1975 by
Gerald Duckworth and Co. Ltd.
The Old Piano Factory
43 Gloucester Crescent
London NW1

Cloth ISBN 7156 0842 8
Paper ISBN 7156 0843 6

Typeset in Great Britain by
Specialised Offset Services Ltd., Liverpool,
and printed by
Unwin Brothers Ltd., Old Woking

Contents

Acknowledgments

This book could not have been written without the help of many friends and former colleagues. Their assistance and advice, and their readiness to put the results of their work — often unpublished — at my disposal, has been unstinted. I am also grateful to all those who have read and commented on the text. My sincere thanks are also due to the curators and staffs of the Cambridge University, Chelmsford, Colchester, Grays Thurrock, Ipswich, Prittlewell Priory, Saffron Walden and Passmore Edwards Museums for the help they gave me while collecting material, and to D.S. Neal for his drawings of the North Hill, Colchester, mosaics which are reproduced in chapter 3. Above all I owe an especial debt of thanks to M.R. Hull, whose work forms the backbone of this book. Finally, but not least, I must thank my husband for his help and patience throughout.

List of Illustrations

Line drawings by Jennifer Gill

1.

Tribal Territory and the Pre-Roman Iron Age

'And further to the east by the Thames estuary are the Trinovantes in whose territory is the town of Camulodunum.' Ptolemy, *Geography ii. 3.*

The surface geology of Essex and south Suffolk is varied, and the differing soils to which this has given rise have profoundly influenced both prehistoric and Roman settlement patterns (fig. 1).[1]

In the north-west is an area of chalk upland, a link in an ancient land route between East Anglia and the Middle Thames basin. This higher land forms a watershed between north-east Hertfordshire and Cambridgeshire on the one side and Essex and Suffolk on the other, and its eastern flank is cut by numerous small rivers, the Deben, Gipping, Stour, Colne, Blackwater and Chelmer. These rivers divide the country into distinct blocks and finally drain through long-winding estuaries into the North Sea. These estuaries opening towards the Continent encouraged early penetration, while their relatively sheltered waters tended to promote communications across them rather than to divide the communities living on their banks. A glance at the map (fig. 1) will show how much easier it must have been in early times to reach the Dengie Peninsula from Tendring Hundred by sea than by land.

Apart from the area between Saffron Walden and Bury St. Edmunds, and a smaller one in south Essex around Grays and Purfleet, the chalk is overlain by chalky Boulder clay. This clay however does not form a continuous sheet; in many places, particularly on the sides of river valleys, patches of underlying glacial gravels and sand outcrop, while to the east around Colchester, Chelmsford and Ipswich the Boulder clay is replaced by glacial loams, sands and gravels. The Boulder

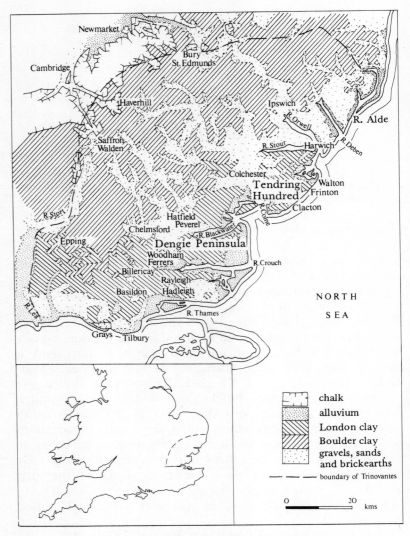

Fig. 1. The geology of the Trinovantian canton

clay itself varies in character. In Suffolk it contains a considerable proportion of Kimmeridge clay, which produces heavy, infertile soils, while further south the Boulder clay is lighter and gives rise to somewhat drier and more easily worked soils, attractive to early settlers.

Over much of east and south Essex the Boulder clay is

replaced by the London Clay belt, a deposit which is on the whole less fertile than the more mixed Boulder clay. The London Clay forms an unbroken sheet over much of central Essex, but in places is capped by beds of pebble, gravel or sand, as at Langdon Hills Basildon, Billericay, Rayleigh and Hadleigh. Where the London Clay is exposed in low cliffs at Harwich, Clacton, Walton and Frinton, seams of septaria, or compacted clay nodules, come to the surface. This provided the only local building stone in the area and was much used in Roman times.

At many places along the coast are broad tracts of recent alluvium, low-lying and generally ill-drained. Most impressive of these are the salt marshes around the estuaries of the Alde and Deben, and those in the Dengie Peninsula of south-east Essex, all areas which still today are often bleak and marshy. The coastline has without doubt altered drastically. Over much of Essex the coast has sunk since Roman times; indeed today stretches of coast between Harwich and Clacton are being rapidly denuded, and there is evidence that this sinkage started in the late Roman period.[2] Further north, around the estuaries of the Deben and Alde, the situation is reversed. Here new land is still being built up through the gradual formation of sand and shingle banks and spits.

On the north bank of the Thames lighter soils re-appear, where gravels and brickearth provided soils attractive to early settlers over a belt some 7-8 km. wide. As with the clays further north, these deposits are in places capped by small areas of sand or gravel (fig. 1).

In Roman times much of Essex and Suffolk must have been forested, and although all that remains today of this primaeval cover is Epping Forest, in 1080, when the Domesday Book was compiled, it still stretched over thousands of acres.[3] There were belts of dense woodland in the area between the Blackwater and the Colne, and another belt running from Hatfield Peverel to Woodham Ferrars; indeed much of the land west of a line between Haverhill and Tilbury was densely forested. In earlier centuries this forest must have been still more extensive.

The Early Iron Age background

The extract quoted at the head of this chapter shows that in Roman times the territory of the Trinovantes stretched at least from *Camulodunum* (Colchester) in north-east Essex to the mouth of the Thames, although the precise boundaries on the north and west are much more difficult to define.

In the pre-Roman period it is highly unlikely that there were fixed boundaries to tribal territories. The 'sphere of influence' of the Trinovantes in the pre-Roman Iron Age must have waxed and waned periodically; it was only in Roman times that the boundaries were stabilised.

The earliest use of iron in this part of East Anglia dates from the seventh to sixth centuries B.C., when scattered iron-using communities appear at West Harling (Norfolk), Creeting St. Mary and Sheepen. The flow of iron-using newcomers gradually increased until by about 500 B.C. a full-scale Iron Age community had emerged. This early pre-Roman Iron Age of Essex and Suffolk was merely a branch of the wider early Iron Age culture which spread right across southern Britain in the last half of the first millennium B.C. Hand-made pottery, incorporating traditions based ultimately on Continental metal prototypes, is found associated with round timber houses which occur both singly and in groups,[4] whose inhabitants practised a mixed farming economy.

At some time in the third or fourth centuries B.C. immigrants from northern France appeared in the area. They introduced new styles of pottery, made in fine dark fabric, often burnished on the exterior, and occasionally decorated with horizontal grooves or with fingertip impressions.[5] This pottery, known as the Darmsden style after the site at which it was first recognised, is sometimes found associated with rectangular houses, which now appear, rarely, for the first time. These new features were gradually absorbed by the indigenous population.

Increasingly as time went on these early Iron Age farmers constructed defended forts, usually on hill-top positions. Presumably, as the Iron Age progressed, the population increased and this, coupled with the inflow of immigrants from the Continent from time to time, resulted in increasing pressure on easily cultivated land. Essex and south Suffolk, however, are basically low-lying areas without pronounced relief, so typical hill-forts are comparatively rare. In the south and west of Essex lies a small group of them (see fig. 2), Loughton Camp and Ambresbury Banks in Epping Forest and Wallbury Camp near Great Hallingbury. No large-scale excavations have been carried out on these forts, but the fort at Ambresbury Banks has been shown to have been first built in the fifth century B.C., although it may have been re-occupied in the Belgic period. Ambresbury Banks covers 11 acres (4.5 ha.), an area which was defended by a rampart and ditch with a small counterscarp bank. The entrance was carefully revetted with dry stone walling. Wallbury, 31 acres (12.5 ha.), was defended in part by a double rampart and ditch, but where marshy ground provided natural defence a single rampart sufficed. Loughton on the other hand is a smaller fort, where 6 acres (2.5 ha.) were defended by a single bank and ditch, while Uphall Camp at Ilford, also surrounded by only one bank and ditch, may well be a post-Roman work. The same applies to the small forts at Prittlewell and South Weald. Finally at Mucking, overlooking the Thames, a small bi-vallate hill-fort, only 75 m. in diameter, has recently been excavated and dated to the fifth century B.C.

In central Essex, seven kilometres east of Chelmsford, lies the hill-fort at Danbury. The site occupies a prominent gravel hill in a generally flat area and commands a fine view over south-east and central Essex. The fort is defended by a single, but still prominent, bank and ditch; until excavations can be organised here, however, its place in the history of Essex must remain largely conjectural.

North-west of Danbury, at Witham, a small fort defended by a single massive rampart and ditch has been shown to date from the Saxon period, probably built by Edward the Elder in the tenth century as part of his scheme of defence against the Danes. The War Ditches at Saffron Walden have also been shown to be post-Roman. The dates of Ring Hill (Littlebury) and Asheldham are uncertain (fig. 2).[6]

It is clear that hill-forts were comparatively rare in the area during the Early Iron Age. There seems to have been a small concentration along the valleys of the Lea and the Stort and

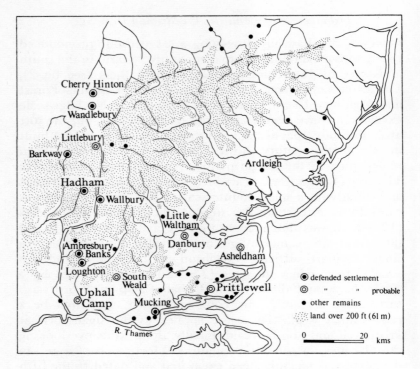

Fig. 2.   Early Iron Age (pre-Belgic) settlement in the canton

their tributaries. In addition to Littlebury, Wallbury and the
Epping Forest forts, forts are known at Little Hadham and
Barkway in Hertfordshire and at Cherry Hinton and Wandlebury in Cambridgeshire, where excavation has shown that the
fort was first built in the third century B.C. It may be that
this area, a natural geographic boundary, was the scene of
conflicts between different groups at some period in the early
Iron Age. Later on a further fort was built on the northern
fringe of our area, at Clare, but this probably resulted from
an attempted expansion by the Trinovantes northwards, in
the first century A.D. (see fig. 3).

It is unlikely that further true hill-forts will be discovered
in the area; they are among the most prominent prehistoric
remains in the country, and by their nature do not pass
unnoticed. It is becoming clear, however, that more humble
occupation sites, single farmsteads or small villages, were
sometimes defended by palisades, or small ramparts and

ditches, as, for example, at Great Stambridge, Mucking and Heybridge. More of these doubtless await discovery.[7]

Although iron was used and manufactured it is seldom found today. Doubtless an expensive commodity, it was carefully looked after and even broken fragments might be re-used by a blacksmith. The sword from Hertford Warren, near Bury St. Edmunds, on the edge of our area, testifies to the skill of the smiths, however, while some of the fine iron daggers found in the Thames may be representative of the equipment used in Essex and Suffolk.[8] A host of other finds, clay loom weights, bronze awls, brooches and pins, indicates the variety of equipment which the inhabitants of Essex and Suffolk had at their disposal, while Professor Cunliffe has suggested that the immigrants who brought with them the Darmsden style of pottery were warriors and horsemen, some of whose remains have been recovered from rich graves in Suffolk and Norfolk.[9]

The early Belgic period

In the last quarter of the second century B.C. a great change in the area was heralded by a renewal of contacts with northern France. Newcomers arrived here bringing with them not only superior skills, but ultimately a more centralised social organisation. They are known as the Belgae.

Britain's first contact with the Belgae, from about 125 B.C. if not before, is represented archaeologically by waves of imported gold coins. The earliest of these have been labelled Gallo-Belgic A and are found sporadically in north Essex and Suffolk.[10] They appear to have been brought here either by Belgic settlers or in the course of trade from the area of north France which lies between the valleys of the Seine and the Somme. They occur mainly in Kent, but some penetrated up the rivers of north Essex and Suffolk where they are sometimes found today.

Shortly after this, about 100 B.C., a fresh wave of gold coins (Gallo-Belgic C) was brought in, this time by Belgic settlers who established themselves permanently in Kent. These new immigrants do not seem to have been able to penetrate into Essex or Suffolk; here presumably the

presence of established tribes prevented them. Consequently
Gallo-Belgic C coins are very rare in our area. Forty or fifty
years after the introduction of Gallo-Belgic C coins, Julius
Caesar conducted his two exploratory British campaigns of
55 and 54 B.C. and in his commentaries the Trinovantes
make their first appearance in the historical record.

Caesar tells us that his principal opponents during his
campaign of 54 B.C., when he was able to press inland, were
the Catuvellauni of Hertfordshire, and his principal allies the
Trinovantes, neighbours and traditional enemies of the
Catuvellauni and until recently the paramount tribe in this
part of Britain. Shortly before Caesar's arrival, however, they
had lost this position when the Catuvellauni had defeated and
killed the Trinovantian king, whose young son, Mandubra-
cius, had then been forced to flee to Caesar for protection.[11]
This brings us to the major question of this chapter. Who
were the Trinovantes, the powerful tribe who allied themselves with Caesar in 54? Can we recognise them in the
archaeological record during the century before the Roman
conquest?

We have already looked at the early pre-Roman Iron Age
in our area in detail because it was against this background
that the Belgic way of life was introduced. The Belgae
brought with them a new and distinctive culture, easily
recognised by the archaeologist. Apart from coins, new metal
types, particularly brooches, were introduced and with them
a new style in art. It is with the Belgic invasions that
wheel-made pottery first made its appearance in this country,
and this fine, hard ware is particularly distinctive. The Belgae
also practised burial customs novel to the native inhabitants,
who at the time had no overall rites of their own. The Belgic
dead were cremated and the ashes, usually buried in flat
cemeteries, were accompanied by grave offerings. Although
the Belgae were not unfamiliar with hill-forts, and indeed
sometimes constructed their own or adapted pre-existing
ones, their most important defended sites were *oppida*, large
tracts of land defended by massive linear dykes, behind
which farmsteads and farmland, pasture and woodland, were
all protected. These *oppida* generally occupied low-lying
positions.

Traces of Belgic occupation have long been known in Kent, where cemeteries originating in the first half of the first century B.C. have been recorded.[12] North of the Thames few Belgic remains are known before the very end of the first century B.C. There is however one major exception. Over the past few years a group of Belgic graves in Hertfordshire and north Essex has been studied by Dr. Stead, all of them graves of unusual, and in a few cases exceptional, richness. Some of the most spectacular examples were found at Welwyn and Welwyn Garden City, and this class of burial has been named the *Welwyn type* after them.[13] In Welwyn type burials the ashes of the dead were accompanied by expensive articles such as can only have been afforded by wealthy families. At Welwyn (Grave B) two splendid cups of Italian workmanship were found, together with pottery, bronzes and remains of an iron frame. At Welwyn Garden City another rich burial produced not only fine pottery and metal work, but also a silver cup, remains of a much repaired wooden gaming board and a magnificent set of twenty-four glass gaming pieces. A slightly later grave in the valley of the Stour in Essex, at Mount Bures, was excavated in the last century and found to contain, among other expensive items, a pair of fine iron fire-dogs. Frequently recurring luxury items in many of the Welwyn type graves are *amphorae* — large storage jars which once contained fine wine and were imported into Britain from vineyards in Campania and southern Italy. These particular *amphorae* are characterised by a collared rim, long, flattened handles and a heavy spindle-shaped body, and are known as Dressel form 1. These have been the subject of a close study by Dr. Peacock, who has been able to show, through petrological analysis of the clay, that the *amphorae* were probably all made in a limited number of Italian vineyards in the second half of the first century B.C.[14] Many of the Dressel 1 *amphorae* in our area come from Welwyn type graves, but others come from less pretentious burials, and still more are preserved in museums, but the details of their find spots and the circumstances of their discovery are not known. Since these are generally complete examples, however, it is considered likely that they also originated in graves. The distribution of Dressel 1 *amphorae* and of

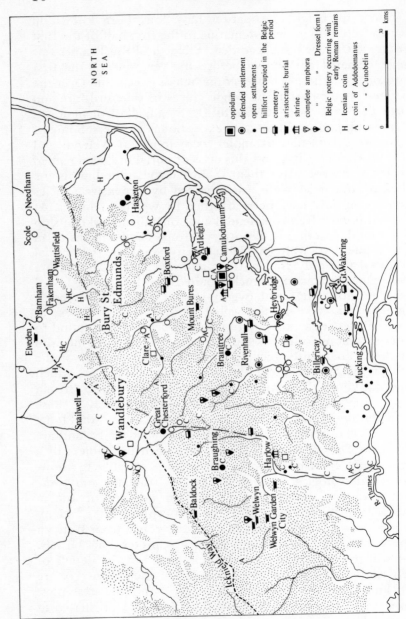

Fig. 3.   Belgic settlement in the canton

Welwyn type graves occupies a band of country from eastern Hertfordshire to Maldon and Colchester on the coast of Essex. To the north the graves spread to the valley of the Stour between Suffolk and Essex, and further west into the southern tip of Cambridgeshire (fig. 3).

Dr. Peacock suggests that these graves represent the territory of the Trinovantes in the fifty years after Caesar's campaigns. He sees them as the graves of wealthy aristocrats who, benefiting from the treaty arrangements between the Trinovantes and Rome, were able to accumulate imported luxuries traded from the Roman world. This distribution of graves and *amphorae*, however, reaches as far west as Welwyn and Wavendon, near Bletchley, lapping into territory that is generally held to have been Catuvellaunian in Roman times rather than Trinovantian. Caesar, however, described the Trinovantes as an extremely powerful tribe in the first century B.C., and, as Peacock has pointed out, we should not be surprised to see correspondingly large territory controlled by the tribe after the departure of Caesar. After 54 the Catuvellauni were bound by treaty not to molest the Trinovantes; it is quite possible that the Trinovantes took advantage of this at the Catuvellauni's expense. *Verulamium*, however, the Catuvellaunian capital after 15 B.C., is just outside the area of the Welwyn graves.

Apart from the Welwyn graves there is little to point to Belgic elements in the area in the first century B.C. It is possible that the Sheepen site, just outside Colchester, was occupied at this date, since, although no structures or defences have been shown to belong to this period, some two dozen fragmentary Dressel 1 *amphorae* have been found here, which suggest occupation on the site by the end of the first century B.C. At Harlow, recent excavations have shown Belgic occupation on the site at the beginning of the first century A.D., possibly starting in the first century B.C.

To the west of the area, an extensive Belgic occupation site is known at Braughing. In the Roman period Braughing must have lain in Catuvellaunian territory, but recent excavations on the site have recovered coins which suggest that at the end of the first century B.C. it was in Trinovantian hands. The pottery from the site includes imported Gallo-Belgic wares, which date from the early part of the first century A.D. and suggest the possibility that Braughing may have been occupied before Sheepen became the major Trinovantian centre.[15]

At the time of writing it looks as if in the first century B.C. the Trinovantes were basically a non-Belgic tribe with only a small Belgic element in it, which formed a richer section, possibly a Belgic aristocracy superimposed on an indigenous tribe of early Iron Age farmers. Thus, although on purely archaeological grounds the Trinovantes who allied themselves with Caesar seem to have been an indigenous tribe, the Welwyn graves suggest that there was already a Belgic element among the Trinovantes in the second half of the first century B.C. How large this element was we cannot tell until much more research has been carried out, particularly on settlement sites. It is possible that these Belgic chieftains came into north Essex shortly before 55 B.C., since Mr. Allen's work on the later Gallo-Belgic coins has shown that there was a further influx of gold coins, Gallo-Belgic E, brought into north Essex by settlers from Belgium and north France, probably shortly before 60 B.C. Were the men who brought these coins later to be buried in the Welwyn type graves?

The Gallo-Belgic E coins are important as they were the last of the waves of imported coins that affected Essex and south Suffolk. Thereafter locally minted coins make their appearance in north Essex in the second half of the first century B.C. To begin with, the inhabitants of Essex and south Suffolk produced small quantities of varying coinages, but by about 15 B.C. the current ruler in north Essex, Addedomarus, issued coins inscribed with his name. Shortly before this date the ruler of the Catuvellauni, Tasciovanus, had started to inscribe his coins, not only with his name but also with that of his capital, *Verulamium*, where his coins were minted. From now on the history of the local dynasties becomes clearer. The inscribed coins suggest that the political situation among the tribes of south-east England, in the last decades of the first century B.C. and the first decade of the first century A.D., was a turbulent one. For a short period, perhaps in 17 B.C., Addedomarus seems to have been ousted from his kingdom by Tasciovanus, who minted a few coins inscribed with his name and the mint mark *CAMV*, the shortened version of *Camulodunum* (Colchester), the site which, in later years at any rate, was the Trinovantian capital. Tasciovanus did not remain at *Camulodunum* long; his coins with this mint mark are correspondingly rare. Addedomarus returned, only to be supplanted some years later by Dubnovellaunus, formerly king of Kent, who either succeeded on the death of Addedomarus, or drove him out of his kingdom. By A.D. 7, however, Dubnovellaunus himself had been driven out, perhaps by Tasciovanus' son Cunobelin. The emperor Augustus records in his *Res Gestae*, last revised in that year, that Dubnovellaunus had fled to him as an exile and suppliant. Clearly tribal boundaries in Britain fluctuated greatly in this period according to the power of individual rulers.

In addition to the coin evidence already described, excavations have shown that there was an increase in Belgic material, especially pottery, in our area in the first century A.D. This pottery is typically Belgic, superior wheel-made vessels in a variety of forms, of which the main ones are pedestal jars, butt beakers, conical and corrugated urns and S-shaped bowls, sometimes with lids.[16] Gallo-Belgic pottery, fine black and red tableware imported from Roman Gaul, also makes its appearance here for the first time.

Much of the Belgic material at present at our disposal was found in cremation cemeteries. It is clear that the influx of Belgic pottery does not merely reflect trade links between the Trinovantes and the Belgic tribes in Kent, but an actual influx of Belgic settlers, practising a new burial rite as well as bringing in new pottery and other equipment. We have already seen how the Welwyn type graves may reflect a Belgic aristocracy in the first century B.C., but in the early first century A.D., Belgic cremation cemeteries appear widely in the area (fig. 3). Over a dozen are known, in some of which the number of graves discovered was not recorded. Lexden (17 graves) was the largest known cemetery (below, p. 27); others include Boxford 1 (7 graves), Boxford 2 (6), Hatfield Peverel (6), Ardleigh (3) and Great Wakering (3). In addition there are a number of isolated Belgic cremation burials:[17]

It is at once obvious that these cemeteries do not indicate large communities.[18] The appearance of women and children in them (at Lexden, Boxford, Billericay and Shoebury) suggests that it was not simply a rite which was confined to male leaders, but that people of all ages and both sexes could be afforded this sort of burial, and indeed, with the exception of Lexden, these little cemeteries have the appearance of family burial places.

This brings us to the two crucial questions about the Belgic settlers. Firstly, how many newcomers were involved; were there just a few warriors and their families or was there an 'invasion' on a larger scale? Secondly, what were the relations between the new arrivals and the pre-existing population?

It is very unfortunate that few Belgic occupation sites in our area have been fully excavated, although several are known to exist (fig. 3). If more sites could be fully excavated, particularly sites which have both pre-Belgic and Belgic occupation, we should be in a better position to assess the relationship between newcomers and indigenous population. Until then we can only guess at the social relations between the two peoples.

The available evidence at the moment is conflicting. At Braintree, Kelvedon, Heybridge and Boxford there seems to be no earlier settlement and new land was opened up in the Belgic period. On the other hand at several sites, among them Canewdon, Shoebury, Asheldham, Mucking, Dunmow, Witham, Little Waltham and Norsey Wood, Billericay, there are clear signs of earlier Iron Age occupation and there may have been a degree of continuity. Similarly the small size of the cemeteries implies rather small farmsteads, perhaps of the type encountered by Caesar in Belgic Kent. On the other hand, several sites in our area, for example Kelvedon, Braintree and Hasketon, have each produced a large quantity of Belgic material covering a wide area and suggesting much larger settlements. Thus there was clearly a variety of settlement types in our area, some of them undefended, some, as at Heybridge, provided with a protective rampart and ditch, or as at Little Waltham, with a palisade. Until more excavation can be carried out, however, much must remain speculation. In general, the distribution map suggests that in the Belgic period, as in the earlier Iron Age, the dense woodland was on the whole avoided, and settlement concentrated in the river valleys (fig. 3). The impression, by and large, is one of co-existence rather than enslavement of the local population by the Belgae.

Cunobelin and Camulodunum

Tasciovanus died in about A.D. 7 and was succeeded by his son Cunobelin, who may have been responsible for the overthrow of Dubnovellaunus. Indeed, the absorption of the Trinovantian kingdom into the Catuvellaunian seems to have been Cunobelin's first action in a reign remarkable for its expansionism. From the beginning of his reign Cunobelin is found minting coins not, as one would expect, at the Catuvellaunian capital at *Verulamium*, but at Trinovantian *Camulodunum* (fig. 4). Not only do we have a series of coins bearing Cunobelin's name on the obverse, and the mint mark for *Camulodunum* on the reverse, but many fragments of clay moulds, in which the blanks for coins such as these could be cast, have been found on the Sheepen site. It is now generally accepted that immediately after his father's death Cunobelin overran the Trinovantes and then moved the Catuvellaunian capital to the Trinovantian centre.

More is known of Cunobelin and his life than of any other British character so far encountered. Described on some of his coins as the son of Tasciovanus, he succeeded his father in *c*. A.D. 7 and, as we have just seen, quickly established himself at *Camulodunum*. For a short time rulers inscribing their coins Sego, Rues, Andoco and Dias, probably colleagues or associates of Tasciovanus, minted coins at Verulamium, but by *c*. A.D. 10 Cunobelin was sole ruler of both the Trinovantian and Catuvellaunian territories. It was not long before he also overran Kent — coins of Cunobelin are found here from *c*. A.D. 25 onwards.[19]

The centre of Cunobelin's kingdom, which by the end of his reign had expanded to cover most of south-east England, lay at *Camulodunum*. Under Cunobelin *Camulodunum*, the *dunum* or fortress of Camulos, a Celtic war god, became the largest and best defended *oppidum* yet known from this

Fig. 4.   A coin of Cunobelin minted at *Camulodunum*

country, and covered in all 12½ square miles (32.5 square km.).

It is clear nonetheless that some parts of this vast site had been occupied long before the advent of the Belgae. At Sheepen, a remarkable site on a hillside 1 km. west of the Roman and mediaeval town of Colchester, occupation existed sporadically from the early Bronze Age.[20] Only 3 km. south-west of Sheepen, on a small gravel spur overlooking the Roman river, lies the Gosbecks site. Here again Iron Age material has been found which probably pre-dates the arrival of the Belgae (fig. 6).

The earliest Belgic influence at *Camulodunum* dates from the second half of the first century B.C., with the appearance of the Dressel form 1 *amphorae*. The large number of these expensive luxuries must indicate unusually wealthy inhabitants of the Sheepen site. Although as yet no defences or structures have been recognised before the first century A.D., the evidence of the *amphorae* for still earlier settlement here is reinforced by the coins of Tasciovanus, minted here in 17 B.C.

One and a half km. south-west of Sheepen are the remains of a rich Belgic cemetery at Lexden. Many of the graves, together with the remains of the early Roman cemetery that later occupied the site, were found during the building of the

Victorian suburb of Colchester which now covers the area. One of the graves in the Belgic cemetery was surmounted by a large earthen *tumulus*, which can still be seen in Fitzwalter Road. This was partially excavated in 1924 by Captain Laver.[21] *Tumuli* occur only rarely in Belgic Britain and it is clear that they were reserved for men of unusual importance; it is not surprising that the 1924 excavations revealed a burial of exceptional richness.

There is some evidence that the *tumulus* had been opened in the past and many of the richest grave goods may already have been taken, but beneath the centre of the mound was found a collection of unique interest, the personal belongings of the buried man. The focal point of the burial seems to have been a large funeral palanquin. This was mainly timber built, and little of it now remains, apart from four iron hoops. As Mr. Hull pointed out, these are not tyres from chariot wheels as was suggested at first, as for most of their circumference they are of square, not flat, section and so would be of no use for wheel bindings. Two iron ferrules, or hollow butts, were found in the same area, and these, Hull suggested, may have come from the object's feet, while the numerous decorative iron and bronze rivets that accompanied the remains indicate how elaborate the bier must once have been.

There were also traces of a large iron-bound chest, again decorated with ornamental bronze rivets, but this had been smashed into numerous fragments and could not be restored. In the south-east corner of the burial area were the hacked-up remains of iron chain mail, which had originally been riveted to a backing, probably of leather, but like so many of the finds in the grave had been broken up into small fragments. This breaking may have been part of the burial ritual, a symbolic killing of the funeral offering, but it may equally have been the work of grave robbers.

Besides the chain mail were still more remarkable finds, including the remains of a garment woven in gold wire. Again, although a large quantity survived, sufficient to suggest a cloak or tunic, it had been so broken up that it was impossible to restore. Rather better preserved was a collection of bronzes, imported from the Roman world. These consisted of the head of a stylised griffin, a small bronze boar, a bronze cupid and small stand or table with ornamental legs (fig. 5). In addition there were two spectacular silver finds. One was a pair of remarkable life-sized models of ears of barley, realistically and delicately modelled in solid silver. Perhaps these were symbolic emblems or regalia; they are reminiscent of the ears of barley portrayed on Cunobelin's coins and may have had a ritual significance. Perhaps they were part of a ceremonial head-dress or breastplate. The second silver object has been seen as the most significant find in the burial. Lying near the centre of the burial area was a silver medallion of the emperor Augustus, struck in 17 B.C., and set in a bronze mount. The entire object is undoubted Roman work but it is not the type of thing one would expect to reach Britain in the course of normal trade. It has been seen instead as a diplomatic gift from Rome to an important Briton, presumably a member of the royal Trinovantian house if not the king himself.

Who was it who was afforded this magnificent burial, rich in comparison with the Welwyn type graves, even after the attentions of grave robbers? No human remains were found apart from a few crumbs of cremated bone scattered over the burial area. This again may be due to the grave robbers, but it means that we do not even know the sex or age of the person buried here. Pottery was scarce but remains of 15 *amphorae* were found. Besides telling us that an enormous quantity of wine was buried in this grave, four of the *amphorae* were of Dressel form 1 and provide a date in, or after, the later part of the first century B.C. for the whole group. The Augustus medallion however, minted in 17 B.C., shows that the burial cannot have taken place before the very end of the century, if not later.

Clearly the person buried here was a man of considerable importance and one of sufficient power and prestige to merit the gift of the Augustus medallion. A member of the local ruling family is the obvious candidate. Until recently it was thought that the grave might have been that of Cunobelin himself, who died in c. A.D. 40, but Dr. Peacock's work on the *amphorae* has shown that the actual date could be 40 years or so earlier and Addedomarus has become a possible

Fig. 5.   Selected finds from the *tumulus* in Fitzwalter Road, Colchester,
including two silver ears of barley (centre rear), and the
Augustus medallion (centre front)

contender. If he was not exiled by Dubnovellaunus he may
well have died at *Camulodunum* at sometime around A.D. 1.

The defences of Camulodunum

Cunobelin transformed the ancient settlement at *Camulodunum* into an immense *oppidum*, defended by massive
linear dykes unparalleled in strength elsewhere in Britain.
These defences have for many years formed a subject of
special study by Professor Hawkes and the following account
is based on his work.

The earliest rampart defence in the whole elaborate
scheme is the Heath Farm Dyke (fig. 6). As a curvilinear
contour work it differs strikingly from the later, straight
defences. It runs around the north, west and south sides of a
small promontory in the gravel plateau overlooking the
Roman river, and occupied by the Gosbecks site. As we have
already seen, this site was occupied in the pre-Belgic Iron
Age, but it continued to be a site of exceptional importance

in the Belgic period and indeed right through the Roman period. It alone was defended by the Heath Farm Dyke, which suggests that this was an area of early importance. It is unfortunate that other than recognising its early place in the defensive system we cannot yet give this dyke a precise date; it may have been the work of Cunobelin, or it may well be earlier and date from the time of Addedomarus, or even to the pre-Belgic Iron Age. Certainly the site continued to be of great importance in the Belgic period, as two of the major dykes of Cunobelin's system make special detours to include Gosbecks. It is clear that in the Belgic period, and perhaps also earlier, the site's importance was religious. Mr. Hull, excavating in the Cheshunt field in 1948-50, discovered a 55 m. square enclosure, delimited by a massive ditch 11 m. wide and 4 m. deep. Hull dated this ditch to the Belgic period on the admittedly slender evidence of a coin of Cunobelin in the primary silt, and the fact that Roman pottery only appeared on the site after about a metre of silt had accumulated in the ditch. Whatever the initial date of the enclosure, however, it was clearly an important sacred site by about A.D. 100 when a substantial Romano-Celtic temple was built in the south-west corner and the ditch surrounded by three parallel masonry walls. Both temple and walls were enclosed in a large *temenos* which dominated an extensive fair-ground, to be described in chapter 4.

The nucleus of the Belgic *oppidum* lay at Sheepen, which Cunobelin defended by three widely spaced ramparts. The innermost of these is the Sheepen Dyke, a massive work, of which only the filled-in ditch remains, defending Sheepen Hill itself. The ditch was over 3 m. deep, approximately 12 m. wide at the top and with a deep V-shaped profile. About 1 km. west of Sheepen Hill is the Lexden Dyke, a long linear work covering 2.5 km. and extending north of the Colne, and perhaps originally also continuing further south and east. Another kilometre west again is a third dyke, the Shrub End Dyke; like the Sheepen Dyke both the Lexden and Shrub End Dykes had massive V-shaped ditches, and originally correspondingly strong ramparts, although today these are naturally much weathered. There is evidence of wooden gateways through both the Sheepen and the Lexden Dykes and a

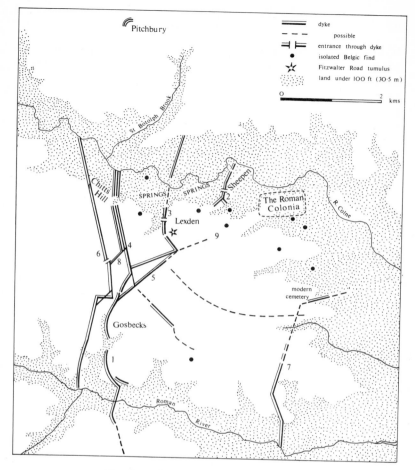

Fig. 6.   The *Camulodunum* dykes

1 Heath Farm Dyke
2 Sheepen Dyke
3 Lexden Dyke
4 Shrub End/Triple Dyke
5 Prettygate Dyke

6 Grimes Dyke
7 Berechurch Dyke
8 Peartree Dyke
9 Colchester Royal Grammar School

suggestion of a timber palisade along the crest of the rampart at Lexden. Finally traces of a fourth dyke, the Barn Hall Dyke, run south and east of the Shrub End and Lexden Dykes.

These four dykes defended the Sheepen area from the west and south and must be early in the sequence of the defences, and the numerous gaps, although possibly originally filled by

dense forest or impenetrable marsh, may equally indicate
that the scheme was never completed. The four dykes
exclude the Gosbecks site and certainly a change of plan is
indicated by the construction of the Prettygate Dyke. This
awkward-looking work connects the south ends of the
Lexden and the Shrub End Dykes with the earlier Heath
Farm Dyke, which is thus rather clumsily drawn into the
system. This inclusion was clearly an after-thought; the Shrub
End Dyke could perfectly well have been built further west,
the older defence included in the scheme, and the re-entrant
angle caused by the Prettygate Dyke avoided. The lie of the
land here is flat and open and no geographical consideration
determined the line of either the Prettygate or the Shrub End
Dyke. Clearly the Prettygate Dyke was a later addition
designed to bring the site at Gosbecks into the defended area.

After one or two minor improvements to the Prettygate
Dyke, the whole scheme was rounded off by the construction
of the immense Grimes Dyke, a prodigious work stretching
for over 5 km. with a rampart that in places still stands over 2
m. high. It formed the outermost western defence, but even
this deviated 200 m. in order to include the Gosbecks site
within its line.

These five defence lines form between them what is in
effect a massive promontory fort, defended on the north and
east by the Colne and its attendant marshes, on the west by
the dykes and on the south by the Roman river. The valley of
the Roman river is smaller than that of the Colne, and it may
have been thought necessary to provide extra, artificial
defences on this side of the *oppidum* in the form of
Berechurch Dyke. Reports of early Saxon pottery from the
body of the rampart, however, raise the question whether it
is post-Roman rather than Belgic. Even if it should prove one
day to be definitely pre-Roman it has never been recorded
west of the cemetery and it is quite likely that it was never
completed.

North of the Colne, just outside the village of West
Bergholt, lies the small hill-fort at Pitchbury. This is a
bi-vallate fort whose defences still stand on the western side,
but which may never have been completed. Since so little of
the fort remains, it is difficult to estimate its size. Although

technically a hill-fort, it is hemmed in on all sides by higher ground and commands no extensive view. One would have thought that it could have been easily taken by surprise. It is difficult to date this earthwork, because it seems never to have been occupied. In 1936 two sections were cut across the western side of the fort, and in 1968 the western part of the interior was cut by a close grid of field drains and watched by archaeologists. No trace of occupation was found in these excavations, which has lent weight to Professor Hawkes' theory that Pitchbury should not be included in the pre-Belgic period at all but that it formed part of the Belgic defensive system for *Camulodunum* and was never actually occupied. However, pottery fragments found when the site was cut by a gas main in 1973 suggest once again that it may date from the very earliest phases of the Iron Age and therefore have little or nothing to do with the Belgic scheme.[22]

Sheepen Hill

We will now turn from the defences of *Camulodunum* to look at the large tract of land they were designed to defend. Belgic finds occur sporadically over most of the 32.5 sq. km. south of the Colne, but a very high proportion of this area must have been given over to woodland (providing pannage for swine), pasture and arable land. In Cunobelin's reign the main occupation was centred on Sheepen Hill.

The gentle slope of Sheepen Hill is cut off from the gravel ridge, on which modern Colchester stands, by a steep-sided if small valley just north of the main London road. Sheepen Hill rises above the marshes of the Colne Valley, commanding an ancient ford across the river. It is conveniently supplied with fresh water from the Sheepen springs on the west, but is itself well drained and relatively sheltered.

Two large-scale excavations have been carried out on this hill. The first, in 1930-9, was undertaken before the construction of the Colchester bypass over the northern end of the site, when much time was necessarily spent in sorting out the defences and in the elucidation of the history of the area as a whole. In 1970 another large area was examined on the lower slope of the hill, prior to its destruction by levelling. Other rather smaller excavations have been undertaken; on the south face of the hill west of Sussex Road in 1971, and on the many Roman kilns on both sides of the hill in the 1930s and the 1950s. Altogether a large proportion of the Sheepen site has therefore been excavated, indeed, probably a higher proportion of the occupied area within an *oppidum* than has so far been possible elsewhere in the country.

Finds have been reported from Sheepen Hill since the mid nineteenth century. It is now clear however, that the bulk of these should be attributed not to the Belgic settlement but to the occupation which existed here in the early Roman period. In spite of the very extensive excavations which have been carried out on the north slope of the hill, fewer than twenty huts have been found which can definitely be said to pre-date the Roman conquest. There is no doubt that more once existed which were later destroyed either during the Roman period, or by post-mediaeval gravel extraction. Nevertheless, we are left with the inescapable conclusion that even the Sheepen site, nucleus of Cunobelin's *oppidum*, was never densely built over. If we bear in mind that one family would doubtless occupy two or three of the small circular huts we must assume that the hill was occupied by only a few scattered homesteads. Most of the huts found so far have been fairly humble structures: small circular or sub-rectangular huts ranging from only 2.5 to 6 m. in diameter (fig. 7). The floors were generally simply of trampled clay, sometimes sunk a few centimetres below the contemporary ground surfaces, and in many cases the walls seem to have been clay-built also, although in some cases the more familiar post holes or sleeper beams were found, all that remains of timber walls. The roofs were presumably thatched in either reed or straw. Occasionally remains of hearths were found in the centre of the floors, while outside the huts were the family rubbish pits. One hut, found in the 1930s under what is today the North East Essex Technical College, had been totally destroyed soon after the Roman invasion; it had apparently been singled out for this thorough destruction, which was by no means the usual treatment. Presumably it

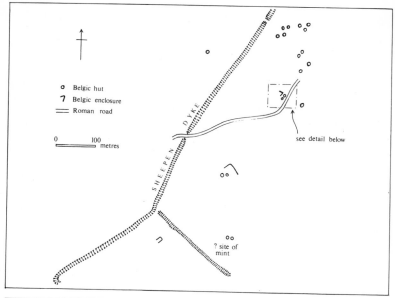

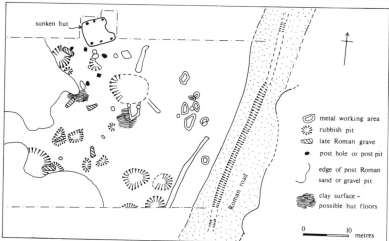

Fig. 7.   Plan of part of the Sheepen excavations, 1970

was the home of someone of particular importance, a suggestion which is supported by the finds in the rubbish pits which surrounded the hut. Six rubbish pits were found, all of them neatly and tidily cut, but their contents, household rubbish doubtless thrown out from the neighbouring hut, included a remarkably high proportion of expensive imported pottery and glass from the Roman world. The pottery, particularly the fine Arretine ware, occurred in quantities much larger than one would expect from an ordinary household. This led the excavators to suggest that the hut might have been the home of Cunobelin himself. At any rate it demonstrates that even people of the wealth implied by the contents of the rubbish pits still lived in simple huts, in no way different from many in the pre-Belgic Iron Age.

Remains of larger buildings have also been found, including part of a large timber structure resting on timber sleeper beams and lying outside the Sheepen Dyke. Rectilinear structures are also suggested by the discovery in the 1930s of a sub-rectangular enclosure measuring 37 m. by at least 10 m. and resting on sleeper beams. In 1970 five large post pits were excavated, all a metre or more in diameter and capable of holding substantial uprights. The post pits were arranged in two straight lines and although the contemporary ground surface had been eroded away they could be securely dated to the pre-Roman period. It is possible that these post pits formed part of a rectilinear timber structure, but they could equally well be part of a cattle compound or enclosure. Unfortunately both lines of pits had been truncated by a post-mediaeval gravel pit.

The inhabitants of the Sheepen site were evidently well-to-do even if few in number. Although their living quarters were rather squalid, their material possessions were frequently expensive, and on occasion magnificent. Examples of imported pottery from Italy and Gaul — Arretine ware, *amphorae* and Gallo-Belgic ware — are by no means uncommon finds, while imitations of Gallo-Belgic wares and certain types of butt beakers occur so frequently as to suggest that they were made on the site. Quantities of metal objects, including a fine enamel terret and fragments of an iron fire-dog, point to considerable luxury, and are eloquent of the wealth of some of the inhabitants of Cunobelin's *oppidum*.[23]

Lexden

Further evidence of this wealth and luxury comes from the Belgic cemetery at Lexden. We have already looked at one princely burial in detail, the tumulus excavated in 1924, but although the most magnificent, it was only one in an extensive Belgic cemetery. Several of the seventeen known graves were found during building operations in the last century and although local collectors at the time kept much of the pottery which is today in the Colchester and Essex Museum, only a few grave groups have been preserved intact.[24] The material remaining speaks of wealth and comfort. In one grave a woman had been buried with her bronze mirror and a bronze cup decorated with coral; nearby a man was equipped with pottery and a bronze tankard or bucket. In a third instance a nobleman went to the grave accompanied by a complete *amphora*, presumably once full of wine. Several complete *amphorae*, one of them of Dressel form 1, have been found at different spots in Lexden; they are all likely to have come from graves. A bronze bust of the emperor Gaius (Caligula) was found many years ago in Colchester. It too may possibly come from a Belgic grave.[25]

Further scattered homesteads must have existed within Cunobelin's *oppidum*, but are yet to be discovered. The Sheepen householders however seem to have formed the upper class. Somewhere must have lived the hundreds of men and women needed to build the massive dykes. Some may have been captives acquired through Cunobelin's expansionist policies, but others must have been Trinovantian peasants, perhaps working on the dykes for part of the year only and returning to their homes to till the land and harvest the crops.

The boundaries of the Trinovantian canton

The appearance, in about 15 B.C., of inscribed coins enables us to make some estimate as to the extent of the Trinovantian territory. There is a small concentration of coins of Addedomarus in the upper Thames basin, although the significance of this is by no means clear. Apart from this Addedomarus' coins occupy a band of country from north-

east Essex to northern Hertfordshire, and the south-east tip
of Cambridgeshire.

Southern Essex poses an interesting problem. A glance at
the map (fig. 3) shows that coins of Addedomarus and
Cunobelin are very rare in south-east Essex. This part of the
county is not particularly attractive land for early settlement,
but was certainly occupied in the Belgic period, as the
distribution of other Belgic finds demonstrates. Indeed, the
distribution of Addedomarus' coins agrees closely with that
of the Dressel form 1 *amphorae* and the Welwyn type graves.
The band of country from north Essex west into north-east
Hertfordshire and the southern tip of Cambridgeshire
emerges as the Trinovantian heartland. At Harlow, on the
other hand, recent excavations and chance finds have
produced some 329 pre-Roman coins, including fourteen
gold examples. Many of these had been deliberately buried,
presumably from religious motives, on the site of the Harlow
temple (below, p. 115), but at least three different sites are
involved. The coins suggest that in the reign of Tasciovanus,
Harlow lay within the Catuvellaunian 'sphere of influence'
rather than the Trinovantian. Thus although in the Roman
period, south Essex, and west Essex including Harlow,
probably lay in the Trinovantian canton, it may not have
done so before the reign of Cunobelin.[26]

To the north the Addedomarus coins share a common
boundary with the Belgic pottery, and it is clear that the
Trinovantian territory never extended north of an imaginary
line drawn through Bury St. Edmunds to Hasketon. It is true
that the map (fig. 3) shows a small belt of Belgic finds further
north, along the valleys of the Little Ouse and Waveney.
Professor Frere, however, has pointed out that the Belgic
material at Needham did not reach the site until the Roman
conquest and the same may well be true of the Belgic
material at Barnham, Fakenham and Wattisfield. The Belgic
tazza at Westhall and bowl at Redgrave are more obviously
strays. This leaves two rich burials at Snailwell and Elveden,
both of which may be evidence of Belgic encroachment on
Icenian territory. Such encroachment however may have only
been temporary. The distribution of both Trinovantian and
Icenian coins shows that the border between the two tribes

must have lain along the watershed between the river systems of Essex and south Suffolk and of Cambridgeshire.[27] The refortification of the hill-fort at Wandlebury at the end of the first century B.C., and the construction of the fort at Clare Castle, may reflect Icenian precautions against Trinovantian expansion northwards.

The western frontier is much more difficult to define. Doubtless it fluctuated considerably in the course of inter-tribal wars. The Lea and Stort valleys may always have been a disputed area in the early Iron Age; we have already seen how a string of hill-forts was constructed at Loughton, Ambresbury Banks, Wallbury, Little Hadham, Barkway and Littlebury in the pre-Belgic period. The coins of Addedomarus and the Welwyn type graves, however, strongly suggest that in the second half of the first century B.C. the Trinovantian territory spread west into Hertfordshire and that the Catuvellaunian *oppidum* at Wheathampstead was near the frontier. Under Cunobelin, when the two tribes were united, this border would have lost its significance.

As we shall see in the next chapter, after the Roman conquest the western frontier was stabilised, probably using the geographical division of the Lea, Stort and Cam valleys.

Summary

The Trinovantes first appear in the historical record in 54 B.C. when they were mentioned by Julius Caesar; archaeology suggests that at the time the tribe was mainly composed of indigenous early Iron Age farmers, although the Gallo-Belgic coins and the Welwyn type graves indicate that there was also a Belgic element, possibly a ruling class of warriors or adventurers recently arrived from northern France and Belgium.

The increase of Belgic material in our area in the first century A.D. underlines the connection between Belgic Kent and Essex which is also suggested by the presence here of the Kentish king, Dubnovellaunus. The large number of Belgic finds need not necessarily reflect a correspondingly large influx of Belgic settlers. The contemporary cemeteries with Belgic pottery are small, but until more settlement sites are excavated the number of Belgic immigrants and their relationship with the pre-existing tribe must remain speculative. At the moment the available evidence suggests that there was only a small number of newcomers who settled side by side with the pre-existing population, who in turn gradually adopted Belgic pottery and customs.

Under Cunobelin the Catuvellauni and the Trinovantes were merged and the great *oppidum* at *Camulodunum* entered its *floruit*, but in spite of the concentration of wealth at *Camulodunum*, it is certain that other wealthy settlements existed in the territory. Extensive Belgic settlements are known for instance at Kelvedon, Braintree, and Hasketon. Nor was *Camulodunum* alone in enjoying luxuries. A number of fine bronze mirrors are known from the area, at Billericay, Great Chesterford, Rivenhall and Mucking as well as from Colchester, and all date from the Belgic period.[28] Most magnificent of all, however, are the six gold torcs which were buried in a hoard on the outskirts of Ipswich. All were beautifully decorated, but four were clearly unfinished when they were hidden. Nevertheless it has been argued that all the torcs came from the area of north-west Norfolk where sixty-five other torcs have been discovered, some twenty-five of them in gold or electrum.[29] On the other hand, if the Ipswich torcs were made in a local workshop, as their unfinished state suggests, they indicate a corresponding degree of wealth, not to mention skill in gold-working, among the Trinovantes in the Belgic period.

Events were to show that Cunobelin's large kingdom, and in particular his *oppidum* at Colchester with its massive defences, and the vast labour expended on constructing the dykes, were to be no match for the Roman army. In A.D. 40 Cunobelin died and his vast territory was divided between his two remaining sons, Togodumnus and Caratacus. Unlike their father they made the mistake of provoking the Romans, who for many years had been toying with the idea of invading Britain. The death of Cunobelin virtually marks the end of independent Belgic Britain; whereas Cunobelin, doubtless through skilled diplomacy, enjoyed a reign of nearly forty years, his less cautious sons ruled for only three. In A.D. 43 the emperor Claudius finally launched the invasion of Britain.

2.

History: A. D. 43 - 367

This is not the place to discuss in detail the events which led up to the Roman invasion of Britain in A.D. 43; suffice it to say that the opportunity of invasion was provided in 42 by the flight to Rome of Verica, king of the Atrebates of Sussex. The Atrebatic kingdom was being steadily encroached upon from the north first by Cunobelin and later by his sons. In A.D. 42 the whole kingdom was overrun by Caratacus and Togodumnus, and Verica's subsequent appeal to Claudius provided him with a convenient pretext for invasion in 43.[1]

Although the Roman army landed in Kent, it is clear that, as the largest and the most important settlement in the south-east, *Camulodunum* was the prime objective. The back of the native resistance was broken within a few weeks after a pitched battle fought at a river crossing somewhere in Kent, probably a ford in the Medway near Rochester. Shortly after this, however, the native forces were given a breathing space for several weeks; a respite which seems to have been put to good use by Caratacus, who, after the death of Togodumnus in a minor skirmish, was left the only surviving son of Cunobelin and leader of the British forces.

After their victory in Kent the Roman army advanced to the Thames where it halted to await the arrival of Claudius himself, who journeyed from Italy with his escort and some reinforcements in order to lead his victorious army into *Camulodunum*. This meant that by the time the emperor had arrived and the army was at last able to cross into Essex, Caratacus had been able to reassemble his followers and a second pitched battle took place north of the Thames. The

British were again defeated and Caratacus was forced to flee westwards, ultimately establishing himself among the Silures of south Wales, where he was to harass successive Roman generals for another eight years.

This left Claudius free to satisfy his ambition of entering *Camulodunum* as a conqueror, and there he received the submission of eleven British kings, among them probably the northern neighbours of the Trinovantes, the Iceni and Coritani.

Those tribes who more or less voluntarily submitted to Claudius at *Camulodunum* would have secured for themselves relatively favourable treatment. Some could expect to become *socii* of Rome, dependent tribes supervised by the Romans, but none the less retaining a measure of internal self-rule, and so long as they paid the tribute demanded and indulged in no anti-Roman policies, able to carry on with little interference. The Trinovantes on the other hand were treated in a different way. They were *dedicitii* — defeated enemy people who were completely at the disposal of the Roman authorities and had few, if any, legal rights. Their territory was to be closely garrisoned, and the people themselves heavily taxed and, in some cases, deprived of their land.

The military garrison in the conquest period

Claudius remained in Britain for a mere sixteen days, before returning to Rome. He left his general Aulus Plautius in charge with instructions to subdue the rest of lowland Britain,[2] but by this time the campaigning season of 43 must have been practically over and the autumn advancing; Plautius' first action would have been to decide upon winter quarters for his large army.

The bulk of the army was probably at Colchester, although a substantial proportion may already have been garrisoned in forts in Kent, Hertfordshire and south Essex. Colchester however became the headquarters of the Roman administration for several years after the conquest, and it is likely that a large semi-permanent camp was established here in the winter of 43/4 to house the invasion army, and that subsequently a fortress was founded.

In the 1950s Professor Hawkes excavated 3 km. west of modern Colchester on the site of the Triple Dyke. This consists of three small dykes, which run parallel to each other for 1.6 km. south from the River Colne (fig. 6). Hawkes cut a section across the Triple Dykes on the brow of Chitts Hill overlooking the Colne and found them to be early Roman in date, although they were probably a modification of the Belgic Shrub End Dyke which continues south from the southern end of the Triple Dyke. The Triple Dyke lies 400 m. east of the massive Grimes Dyke and runs parallel to its northern end. Hawkes was able to show that the two were connected 1.6 km south of the river by the east-west Peartree Dyke, an earthwork which was constructed not earlier than the Claudian period.

Thus we have an enormous enclosure delimited by the river Colne on the north, Grimes Dyke on the west, the Peartree Dyke on the south and the Triple Dyke on the east. Local terrain also played its part. Not only did the marshes of the Colne valley form the northern boundary, but excavation by the writer in 1966 showed that the Triple Dyke was absent from the floor of the small valley which runs east from Chitts Hill to the Lexden Springs.

In some respects this enclosure is reminiscent of the Claudian bridgehead at Richborough, used by the invasion army for a very limited period during the landings of 43. Professor Hawkes has suggested that the Chitts Hill enclosure was similarly designed to accommodate large numbers of troops for a short time, perhaps Plautius' army over the winter months of 43/4.[3]

It must be emphasised however that the Chitts Hill enclosure was nothing more than a semi-permanent camp, used for a few months only. The defences, including the Triple Dyke, are of a temporary character, and in spite of intensive modern building operations over much of the area in recent years, no Roman occupation material has been recorded; a circumstance surprising for a semi-permanent fort and surely inconceivable for a permanent fort occupied over several years.

Nevertheless, as already hinted, there must have been a

Fig. 8.   Tombstone of the Thracian cavalryman, Longi

permanent fort at Colchester, almost certainly one of considerable importance. *Camulodunum* had been the centre of the most powerful anti-Roman force in the south-east, and it was destined to become, for a short time, the capital of the Roman province; added to this the mouth of the Colne, with its modern and mediaeval port (their Roman predecessor has yet to be discovered) lies opposite the mouth of the Rhine and the contemporary naval supply base at Valkenburg. Colchester was the obvious place for a major military base.

Tacitus implies that in A.D. 49 the XXth legion was stationed here before it was moved to the Gloucester area, while one of the treasures in the Colchester Museum is the tombstone of the Thracian cavalryman Longinus, who died while a serving soldier, presumably stationed at Colchester, since the tombstone comes from the early Roman cemetery west of the town bordering the main London road (fig. 8).[4]

Tactically the site of Colchester offered the conquerors many advantages. It was linked by sea with both Kent and the Continent; while land communications were good with the rest of East Anglia and the Midlands, where Roman armies were pressing north and west. Reasons which had made *Camulodunum* ideal as a pre-Roman centre made it the obvious pivot for the Roman garrison of the area.

For many years opinions have varied as to where the permanent fort stood, and the site of the Colchester Royal Grammar School was generally the most favoured place, largely on account of the alignment of Roman roads in the vicinity. More recently evidence has been found pointing to a position beneath the west part of the later *colonia*, a site which incidentally has certain natural advantages as it overlooks the lowest ford in the Colne and the native centre at Sheepen. In addition it has easy land communications with the Claudian supply base at Fingringhoe, near the mouth of the Colne.

Excavation in 1971-2 in *insulae* 36 and 37 of the later Roman town by Mr. Crummy revealed a north-south rampart and ditch and parts of several timber buildings, probably barrack blocks, all of pre-Boudiccan date and clearly belonging to an early fort. The ditch *may* be the same work as the ditch found in 1964 and 1967 90 m. south of the north wall

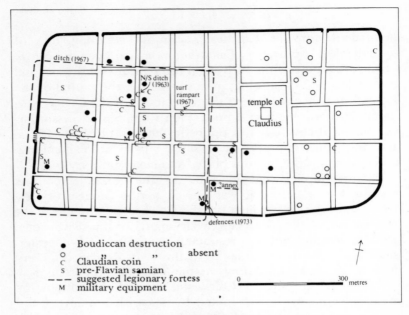

Fig. 9. Pre-Flavian Colchester

of the town. If, as seems likely, the line of the later town wall on the west of the *colonia* roughly corresponds to the west edge of the fort (fig. 9), an area of 50 acres (20 ha.) would have been enclosed by the defences, indicating a fortress capable of accommodating at least an entire legion.[5] Apart from the barrack blocks in *insula* 36, military equipment has been found on three sites within the fortress, all three of them on North Hill, that is the extreme west end of the later town. At two sites small bronze military fittings were found in Claudian rubbish pits, while on the third site over thirty such finds, including a fine dagger in a silver inlaid scabbard, were associated with a timber building of mid first-century date (figs. 10-11). It is now suggested therefore that the *colonia* at Colchester, like the other two first-century *coloniae* in Britain, grew up on the site of an earlier fortress. The fortress at Colchester appears to have been comparatively large, and it may be that some auxiliary troops were brigaded with the legionaries,[6] hence the tombstone of the cavalryman Longinus and the predominance of cavalry equipment on North Hill. On the other hand, the military

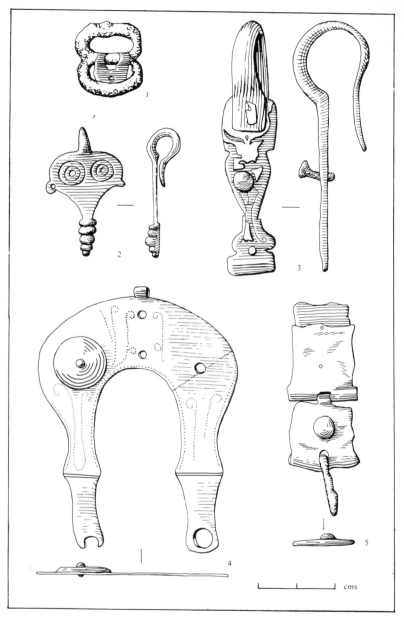

Fig. 10. Military bronzes from North Hill, Colchester

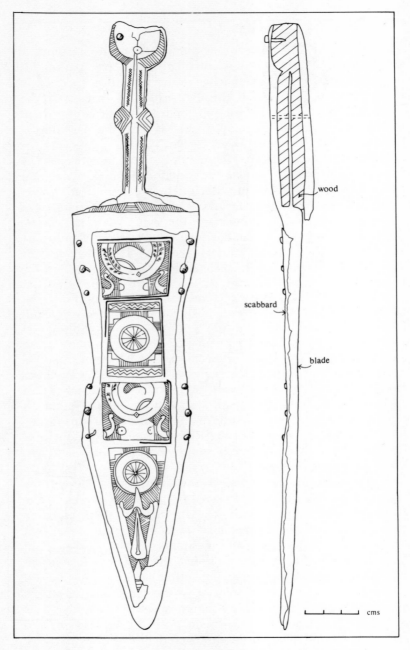

Fig. 11. A dagger in a silver inlaid scabbard from North Hill, Colchester

occupation at Colchester may have had quite a complex history; Mr. Crummy has distinguished two phases of occupation in *insula* 36, and has drawn attention to an early ditch running north-south through *insula* 11 just inside the fortress, and an early turf rampart beneath the street between *insulae* 12 and 20. It may well be that the garrison at Colchester was changed at least once.

One of the most interesting early Roman sites in the canton is the supply base at Fingringhoe, 6 km. downstream from Colchester. The site occupies a pronounced gravel headland, the first high, well-drained piece of mainland that the sailor sees as he comes up the estuary of the Colne through the marshes of the Purfleet and Alresford Creek. The site has now been virtually destroyed by gravel digging, but some information has been gleaned from it. Apart from three villas dating from the later first century, the site has produced a large quantity of Claudian pottery and imitation Claudian coins of the type issued to the Roman army as small change, together with military equipment including a fine camp kettle. These finds seem for the most part to have come from the filling of small rubbish pits set in regular parallel rows, and reminiscent of the rows of rubbish pits sometimes found outside barrack blocks. A military establishment of some sort clearly existed here, and its position, at the mouth of the Colne, suggests a depot or supply base, perhaps linked with forts on the mouth of the Rhine. Fingringhoe compares well with the other Claudian supply bases at Richborough, Fishbourne and Hamworthy.

A glance at the map of the Trinovantian canton shows how central a position Colchester occupies, and how many of the Roman roads radiate from it. Although in their metalled form many of these probably date from the later first century, already in Claudian times a network of tracks would have been essential in order to police the area. Colchester was the pivot of this network, but effective patrolling would depend upon a system of forts or fortlets studding the whole area, and ideally only a day's march apart. So far only a few of these Claudian forts have been positively identified, and although several have been discovered during the intensive archaeological fieldwork that has gone on in our area over the

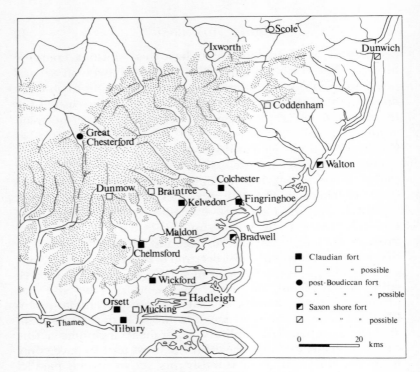

Fig. 12. Military sites in the canton

last few years, many more must await discovery (fig. 12).

At Kelvedon, 14 km. south-west of Colchester along the London road, military small finds and Claudian pottery have been found in the area between the modern village and the river Blackwater. Mrs. Rodwell, in a series of excavations from 1970-2, has traced military ditches associated with Claudian pottery, all of which points to a fort here doubtless superintending the Belgic site we have already mentioned.[7]

At Chelmsford, the late Professor Richmond suggested that a north-south bank on the east side of the Roman settlement was of Claudian date. Recent excavation however has shown that this bank is a natural feature and that the Claudian defences must be sought elsewhere. In 1972 Mr. Drury found evidence of military occupation near the crossing of the river Can by the London-Colchester road, and a Claudian military ditch has been recorded some 200 m. further south, doubtless associated with a fort situated on the slightly higher ground in this area.[8]

Further forts are known from southern Essex. A small rectangular enclosure at Orsett, first noticed some years ago, has now been shown by Mr. Rodwell to be a Claudian fort, covering 2 acres (0.8 ha.) and defended by a rampart and double ditches. At Gun Hill, Tilbury, Mr. Rodwell has recorded another similar fortlet.[9] At Hadleigh, near Great Wakering, a third, commanding a wide view over the mouth of the Thames, is known from aerial photography (fig. 13). Although no excavation has been carried out here, the photograph shows a small square fort with striking similarities to the Neronian signal station at Martinhoe on the north Devon coast. Hadleigh however could equally well have been part of the late Roman Saxon Shore defence system, and only excavation will provide the answer.[10]

A further fort or fortlet was discovered in 1971 by Mr. Rodwell at Wickford. This fort also dates from the Claudian period but the excavator is of the opinion that it was only a temporary fort or marching camp. At Mucking, near Tilbury, and overlooking the Thames estuary, Mrs. Jones has excavated a small rectangular earthwork enclosure which may also be military; it dates from the conquest period, and a military apron mount has been found on the site.[11]

West of Colchester the main road to St. Albans, Stane Street, was likewise garrisoned. At Braintree Belgic and Roman material has been found in some quantity, and recently rescue excavations have been conducted in the modern town centre by Mr. Drury. It is very likely that an early fort lies somewhere near the road junction between Stane Street and the Chelmsford to Great Chesterford road, but so far its exact position has not been established, although its discovery is probably only a matter of time. Similarly at Dunmow, excavation by Mr. Drury has demonstrated Roman occupation on the hill top just west of the modern town centre, though so far no fort has been located.[12]

North of Colchester early military occupation has been suggested at Scole, Norfolk, just north of the boundary between the Trinovantes and the Iceni,[13] while Great Chesterford has produced undisputed evidence for early military occupation, and Mr. Rodwell has recently published

Fig. 13. Aerial photograph of the fortlet at Hadleigh

evidence showing that the fort, lying slightly to the north of the later Roman town, is a very large work of 35-7 acres (14-15 ha.) and so capable of housing at least half a legion. The samian ware found in the fort ditch, and the absence of very early Roman material, however, suggest that this large fort was part of the military re-organisation of the area after the Boudiccan revolt.[14]

It need hardly be stressed how incomplete is our picture of the military occupation of the territory of the Trinovantes after the conquest. If the canton was to be closely policed, forts would have been necessary every 30-40 kilometres along the main routes, and many must remain to be found. The occupation of these forts was often probably short-lived, and the remains may be correspondingly faint. Dr. Webster has stressed the close connection between early forts and small Romano-British towns;[15] it is highly likely that the small settlements at *Combretovium* (where pits containing Claudian pottery and a piece of cavalry equipment have been recorded) and Long Melford will turn out to have succeeded early forts, while at Maldon Mr. Rodwell has noted a small rectangular enclosure, which he suggests may prove to be a conquest-period fort, perhaps supervising the Belgic settlement on the other side of the river at Heybridge.[16]

We shall never know how great a proportion of the tribe's warriors was killed in the battles against the Romans in 43, nor how many survived only to flee west with Caratacus,[17] but the period of military occupation must have been a grim one for the defeated remnants of the tribe left in Essex and Suffolk. Of the remaining able-bodied men in Essex and Suffolk, some at least seem to have been rounded up shortly after the conquest and kept under military supervision in the 'works depot' at *Camulodunum*. Excavation has demonstrated that there was a great increase in population on Sheepen Hill soon after the conquest. In contrast to the scattered occupation pattern in the Belgic period, immediately after the arrival of the Roman army, rows of small workshops were built in which large scale metal-working was carried out. Behind the workshops, relegated to a special zone, were hundreds of rubbish pits, which yielded a mass of domestic and industrial rubbish. The site was crossed by a Roman road, flanked on either side by the metal workers' huts. One of these buildings was found in the 1930s excavations and was of strikingly barrack-like design, but the 1970 excavations suggested that such a building was exceptional, the general rule was for more flimsy buildings of timber and daub, although with open verandahs fronting onto the road in the Roman military style. Unfortunately post-Roman gravel working had destroyed a great deal, but a glance at the plan of the site (fig. 7) shows how the whole area was intensively utilised, indeed the very cramming together of the rubbish pits into their particular zone shows how limited was the waste ground available.[18]

Some of the inhabitants of the workshops may have been natives. The pottery they used was largely native in style; but nevertheless, associated with it, scattered over the floors of the workshops and through the filling of the pits, were numerous pieces of Roman military equipment, bronze buckles, cuirass hooks, fragments of shield binding and pieces of broken helmets, together with dozens of the imitation bronze coins issued to the Roman troops. Clearly the 'works depot' was closely supervised by Roman soldiers, though some of the work was probably undertaken by natives, and it is possible that a small fort stood for a short time at the north end of the 'works depot,' commanding the ford in the Colne, where Sheepen bridge now stands.

The military occupation of the Trinovantian lands was probably never intended to be more than a temporary arrangement. In A.D. 47 we are told that the tribes of the lowland zone were disarmed while two years later in 49 the garrison was largely withdrawn to reinforce the western frontier. Tacitus strongly implies that the XXth legion which arrived in the Gloucester region in the later part of 49 was brought from Colchester.[19] Although we can be sure that the garrison of the Trinovantes was substantially reduced after seven years of occupation, no one would claim that all forts in the canton were totally abandoned immediately; a police network must have been maintained, though perhaps on a much reduced scale. Tacitus tells us that in A.D. 60 there was still a small garrison at Colchester, which was reinforced with a further 200 men from London, and he implies that there were occupied forts elsewhere in the canton.[20]

Civilian arrangements after the conquest

One of the foremost changes that must have affected the civilian life of the Trinovantes would have been the permanent fixing of the tribal boundaries, perhaps during an early census of the new province. We have seen in the first chapter how in pre-Roman times the tribal boundaries probably fluctuated considerably from time to time, but that the heart of the Trinovantian territory lay in north Essex and south Suffolk.

In the Roman period, as in earlier times, the Trinovantes' northern boundary marched with the southern limit of the Icenian canton. The homeland of the Iceni centred on the Breckland of Norfolk and Suffolk, as is shown particularly by the distribution of Icenian coins.[21] These coins are of early Roman date (*c*. A.D. 43-60) and the fact that they are not found south of a line from the Deben to the Little Ouse, except in contexts that can be explained by the dispersal of the tribe after the Boudiccan revolt, indicates that here must run the frontier between the two tribes after the conquest.[22] It may be remembered that in the pre-Roman period neither Belgic pottery nor coins of Tasciovanus or Cunobelin are found north of this line.

Turning now to the south of the canton, we saw in the first chapter how the coins of Addedomarus avoid the area that is now south-east Essex, though Belgic pottery is found there, and we suggested that this land may not always have been part of Trinovantian territory. During the Roman period, however, it was probably part of the canton, and indeed the description of the Trinovantes by Ptolemy 'on the mouth of the Thames' places them precisely here.[23] The Thames forms the natural and obvious boundary between them and the Cantiaci of Kent.

In Roman times, as in the pre-Roman period, the western boundary, separating the Trinovantes from the Catuvellauni, is the most difficult to define. In the pre-Roman period the coins of Cunobelin naturally covered both territories, nor were there precisely distinguishable differences in material culture after the first century B.C. This lack of material on which to differentiate between the two tribes becomes even more acute in the Roman period, and the boundary can only be approximately drawn between the two. In the north-west it is taken to follow the higher land along the chalk escarpment, and in the south, the marshes of the Lea valley, with Harlow and Great Chesterford on the frontier as small market settlements. It must be emphasised, however, that this boundary is a somewhat arbitrary one.

With the reduction of the army in the area, the process of Romanising the Trinovantes and drawing them into the newly formed province was free to go ahead. The focus of the Romanisation was to be at Colchester, where a *colonia* was established in A.D. 49-50.

The *colonia*, a chartered town, was populated by veteran legionaries, all of them Roman citizens and hence enjoying special rights and privileges under Roman law. The colonists at Colchester were probably veterans of the twentieth legion, while according to Tacitus, the idea behind the founding of the *colonia* here was both to provide an example to the surrounding Trinovantes of Roman civilian life in the accepted style, and to form a trained reserve on the spot should the need arise. We shall see in the next chapter the important role that Colchester was to play; suffice it here to say that right from the start the *colonia* was a model town, graced with impressive public buildings and all the amenities of Roman town life.

The new town however was not built without cost, the brunt of which fell on the Trinovantes and which was to have the most severe repercussions.

The *colonia* required a substantial amount of land; it was not simply confined to the 50-60 acres (20-25 ha.) covered by its stre_ts and buildings. A *colonia* was normally provided with a *territorium*; an extensive tract of land surrounding the town and divided up among the colonists so that each would have his own smallholding. As we shall see in a later chapter, the new *colonia* may ultimately have required almost 200 square miles (500 square km.) of land, which was forcibly appropriated from the Trinovantes. Indeed Professor Richmond suggested that in the case of the Trinovantes the land was officially classed as *agri captivi* which meant that instead of being deprived of the land required for the *territorium* outright and at one blow, the colonists were able to appropriate further native land at will, in a continuing process of acquisition.[24]

The sequestration of some of their most fertile land was not the only hardship that the unfortunate Trinovantes had to undergo. The *colonia* itself had to be built, no doubt with forced native labour. Traces of at least one tile kiln of this date have been found on the Sheepen site, and this could well have been supplying the *colonia*. Once built, the expensive public buildings had to be maintained, and foremost among them was the great Temple of Claudius. The temple and the cult of the deified emperor Claudius has recently been the subject of discussion,[25] and it is likely that the enormous temple itself was not built until after Claudius' death and official deification in A.D. 54, although the large altar that stood at the base of the steps that led up to the temple may have been consecrated earlier, possibly to 'Roma and Augustus' rather than to Claudius himself. Certain it is, however, that the construction of the temple threw an extremely heavy burden on the Trinovantes, which the ceremonies connected with both altar and temple only increased.

It is worth while at this stage to consider the contrast in the treatment of the Trinovantes and their neighbours the Catuvellauni. There is no hint anywhere in the written sources that the Catuvellauni were deprived of any of their land, and indeed in the Roman period their canton was among the largest in Britain, containing within its boundaries large areas of fine agricultural land. Nor was this all. The Catuvellauni were granted the added distinction of a *municipium* at *Verulamium*, and Professor Frere has shown that as early as the pre-Flavian period, a regular street grid was making its appearance in the town, while at least one native businessman was investing money in a block of shops built in Roman style.[26] This treatment is in sharp contrast to that meted out to the Trinovantes and indeed this difference may have led to some bitterness between the two tribes. During the Boudiccan revolt, not only did the Catuvellauni apparently take no part, but their fine new *municipium* was attacked by the rebels, and looted and razed to the ground in just the same manner as Colchester and London.

All this surely brings us to one conclusion. To the Roman conquerors the two tribes were distinct; on the one hand were the Trinovantes, resolutely anti-Roman and opposing them all the way to *Camulodunum*. On the other hand were the Catuvellauni, a tribe which must have proved more tractable, and consequently were afforded privileges. How can we explain this difference in treatment? One possibility is that Togodumnus took over the Catuvellaunian territory on the death of Cunobelin, and Caratacus the Trinovantian. In this case, after Togodumnus' death, Catuvellaunian resistance may have petered out, whereas the remaining Trinovantes perhaps acted as scapegoats for Caratacus' prolonged struggle against Rome in the west. This of course is pure speculation, and we shall probably never know for certain why there was a difference in treatment of the two tribes, but marked difference there certainly was and it was soon to lead to grave repercussions.

The Boudiccan revolt

The first result of the Roman treatment of the Trinovantes was neither trivial nor long-delayed. It nearly cost Rome the province. The Boudiccan revolt of 60 must be one of the best known events of the history of Roman Britain, and the Trinovantes were intimately concerned with it.

The events that led up to the rebellion of the Iceni of Norfolk under their queen, Boudicca, are well known, but the reasons that led to the Trinovantes' involvement in the rising were more complex and longstanding.

The natural resentment felt by the Trinovantes over the loss of some of their best land to the colonists was exacerbated by the brutal and rapacious conduct of the settlers themselves, to which the military authorities turned a blind eye, hoping, as Tacitus tells us, 'for similar licence when their own turn came'. The financial burdens occasioned by the construction of the Temple of Claudius added to this chronic resentment, while the sudden calling in of loans made to natives, by the philosopher and speculator Seneca and doubtless others also, merely added fuel to an already smouldering fire.

It is clear that the two tribes chose their moment with care, and much time must have been spent in preparation. In the summer of 60 the Roman governor, Suetonius Paulinus, was campaigning in north Wales with the bulk of the army, thus leaving south-east England with little more than a skeleton garrison. This provided a splendid opportunity to the natives, and as Paulinus was crushing the Druids in their stronghold on Anglesey, the Iceni and Trinovantes rose in revolt.[27]

The first objective of the rebels was the *colonia* at Colchester. This, so Tacitus tells us, had no defences, and archaeology has so far proved him broadly correct.[28] It is clear, however, that there was a small garrison here, which was reinforced, at the urgent request of the colonists, by 200 men sent from London by the procurator Catus Decianus. These 200 were to prove too few. The colonists at Colchester had some warning of their danger; not only did they have time to send for these reinforcements, but Tacitus provides us with lurid descriptions of the omens and portents seen by the inhabitants of the Roman town.

Any precautions that were taken (and Tacitus tells us they were remarkably few) were, however, of no avail. Boudicca and her followers arrived after successfully ambushing the IXth legion, which, at the first news of the revolt, had set out from its base or bases in the east Midlands to intercept the rebels on their way to Colchester. The rebels destroyed the 'works depot' at Sheepen and re-occupied the old native site, which they re-defended with a palisade, closely following the line of the now filled-in Sheepen dyke. On the neighbouring hill the new *colonia* was looted and burnt to the ground. Tacitus tells us that the colonists finally took refuge in the Temple of Claudius; whether or not this was completed in 60 is uncertain, but it is the only completely stone-built structure that we know of in the town at this date, and presumably enough of it was standing to provide some sort of defence. At any rate, the colonists barricaded themselves here, and withstood a siege lasting two days and nights. Finally, however, the rebels prevailed and the defenders were massacred.

The archaeological evidence for the Boudiccan destruction is widespread over the whole of the Claudian *colonia*. The town was virtually razed to the ground. So far no building has been found, dating from the town's earliest phase, which escaped total destruction by fire. At a low level all over the west and central parts of the *colonia* — the area covered by the pre-Flavian town — is a thick layer of clay daub, burnt to a hard bright bed and containing the carbonised remains of beams and posts and even, on occasions, the wattle that formed the core of the lath and plaster walls. The private houses had all been abandoned in haste; the occupants left their goods behind and the burnt daub is nearly always rich in finds for the archaeologist. Two famous samian and glass shops on the town's main street were found in 1927 and 1929 by Mr. Hull, and here the complete wares of the shops, piles of imported glass and expensive samian ware, were left stacked on shelves which had come crashing down from the walls as the building collapsed. In *insula* 10 of the later town a large warehouse, possibly a regional depot of the procurator, had been abandoned with its store-rooms full of corn, *amphorae*, flagons and mortaria. All these were found lying on the floors beneath about a metre of burnt debris. Next door were remains of a lamp shop, and in *insula* 11 part of what must have been a spacious private house. Here were found the charred remains of a human skeleton lying on the floor of the verandah fronting a street. It is curious that in spite of the enormous loss of life during the revolt (Tacitus reports 70,000 killed in *Camulodunum, Londinium*, and *Verulamium*), this is so far the only skeleton reported which can certainly be related to these events.[29]

After the sack of Colchester, Boudicca and her followers may have remained for a few days on Sheepen Hill. We have already mentioned the new palisade defence put up here, but Boudicca's horde would not have taken long to erect so modest a defence.

From Colchester Boudicca moved south. According to Tacitus, she avoided forts and made instead for the large civilian centres at London and *Verulamium*. We cannot yet point with any certainty to forts in Essex or Suffolk which may have been held by a skeleton force. There seems to have been a settlement at Chelmsford at this period, and the masonry bath house recorded by Chancellor in 1949 seems to have been burnt down at about this time. On the other hand, timber buildings overlying the filled in ditch of the Claudian fort escaped burning and were deliberately dismantled when Chelmsford was re-garrisoned after the revolt. Apart from Colchester and Chelmsford, however, traces of the Boudiccan destruction are not definitely proved from the canton. It should be borne in mind that the homesteads of the Trinovantes, who were after all participators in the revolt, may well have escaped destruction.

After Boudicca

Although Paulinus and his army were powerless to prevent the sack of either London or *Verulamium*, Boudicca was finally defeated in the late summer of 60. The defeat was total. Tacitus hints that some bands of rebels held out for several more months, but the death of Boudicca left them without an overall leader, and organised resistance did not survive the holocaust of 80,000 British dead.

Most of the remaining Trinovantes and Iceni must then have been left to find their way home as best they could. The bronze head from a life-sized statue of the emperor Claudius, found in 1907 in the river Alde, Suffolk (fig. 14), was almost certainly loot brought from Colchester. It has been suggested that a returning tribesman threw the head into the river, anxious not to be caught with such incriminating evidence in his possession; alternatively it may have been a votive offering to the river. More recently a Roman helmet, probably a piece of gladiatorial armour, was found at Hawkedon, Suffolk, which was also doubtless spoil from Colchester subsequently hidden to avoid retribution.[30]

The Roman treatment of the defeated rebels was initially very severe. Mr. Allen has shown that the distribution of Icenian coins may be evidence of the dispersal of some of the Iceni, presumably as slaves, after their defeat; although there is no evidence, it is quite conceivable that the ringleaders of the Trinovantes suffered a similar fate. Another obvious step would be the re-garrisoning of the Trinovantes. A fort was again established at Chelmsford after the revolt, while the large fort at Great Chesterford dates from this period also. The forts at Ixworth and Scole on the Trinovantian/Icenian border may well prove to be of similar date and other examples doubtless await discovery.[31]

After the Boudiccan revolt there is no further historical reference to the Trinovantes. No tribal capital bears their name, nor is there documentary or epigraphical mention of them apart from brief references by Dio and Ptolemy. This dearth of evidence must raise the question of whether the Trinovantes survived at all or whether the tribe was finally dispensed with and its territory divided up between the *colonia* and neighbouring tribes.

Fig. 14. Bronze head of Claudius from the river Alde

Such an extreme step as this seems unlikely. Tacitus describes a policy of appeasement after Paulinus' recall, and there is no reason to suppose that the Trinovantes received harsher treatment than the Iceni, who, although sacrificing some of their lands to form an imperial estate around the Fens, and suffering punitive taxation for several generations, nevertheless retained their tribal identity — Caistor by Norwich, founded after the revolt, bears their name. Since it is unlikely that the Trinovantes were worse treated, we may reasonably assume that they too retained their tribal status.

No trace of an imperial estate has been found in the Trinovantian canton, but the tribe may well have suffered punitive taxation. For most of the Roman period much of the canton remained relatively poor, boasting comparatively few very wealthy villas. In spite of taxation, however, the daily life of the Trinovantes must have gradually returned to normal. If the situation among the Trinovantes was anything like that among the Iceni, by about 70 the remaining garrison had probably been withdrawn, and although Colchester recovered only slowly, by the end of the century both the *colonia* and its hinterland were prospering. Nevertheless, by this time London seems to have superseded Colchester as the provincial capital, completing a process which had already started in the pre-Boudiccan phase (below, p. 73). Later, however, Colchester was surrounded by fine masonry defences with impressive gateways, perhaps as early as the mid second century, and before the end of the century, Chelmsford had been given earthwork defences.

There is at Colchester evidence for at least two serious fires destroying large areas in this period and there is also evidence of burning in the Antonine period at several other sites in the canton, including Chelmsford and Kelvedon.[32] Whether these fires were started accidentally or deliberately, and whether they were connected with one another or not, is as yet too early to say, but as the third century advanced there arose in the Channel and North Sea a new danger: that of Saxon pirates. These pirates probably started as a menace to coastal trade and shipping, but later they not only became increasingly dangerous and numerous, but also threatened exposed settlements.

The Saxon Shore

The two large, late Roman coastal forts that are known from the canton, Bradwell-on-Sea (*Othona*) and Walton Castle, were almost certainly built in an attempt to deal with these pirates. They were part of a larger scheme of defence known as the Saxon Shore, which stretched along the southern and eastern coasts of England, from Portchester Castle, overlooking Portsmouth harbour, to Brancaster in Norfolk.

Early in the third century the old-established string of second-century forts in Kent and Sussex was extended with the construction of forts at Reculver and Brancaster, while slightly later in the same century the fort at Burgh Castle (Suffolk) and a small fortlet at Richborough were built. Towards the end of the third century however, possibly under Carausius in *c.* 285, the system of coastal defences was improved and extended to counter the growing danger caused by Saxon pirates. The forts at Richborough, Dover and Lympne were rebuilt at this time, and that at Portchester was founded. Although the dates of both forts in the Trinovantian canton are unknown, they also probably belong to the same period.[33]

The fort at Bradwell lies on the south bank of the river Blackwater, a low-lying and exposed position, but one that commands a wide view along the coast. Unfortunately, as is the case with so much of this stretch of coastline, the site has been much eroded by the sea. Only the western end of what must once have been a substantial fort remains today. Concurrent with coastal erosion is the gradual silting up of the estuary; Bradwell now overlooks a muddy creek, which in Roman times was doubtless a viable harbour.

Compared with those from some other Saxon Shore forts, the remains at Bradwell are not impressive. Indeed they were only discovered, more or less by accident, when the sea wall was being built here in 1864. Excavation the following year established the line of the fort wall where it still survived, that is at the west end, the south-west and north-west corners, and for some 87 m. along the north side and 45 m. along the south. Thus, although the width of the fort is known (157 m.), we have no idea of the original length since the entire eastern end has been obliterated in salt marshes. In addition to this it is clear that the fort's plan was not entirely regular; it broadened out towards the now vanished east end. The walls themselves, 4.2 m. wide at foundation level, are solidly built of septaria with bonding courses of tile, but have been extensively robbed. In most places only the foundations survive and only for a short stretch on the southern side can any of the wall be seen above ground today.

It is uncertain whether or not any of the original gateways survive. On the west wall, 75 m. from the north-west corner, the small Saxon chapel of St. Peter on the Walls lies astride the fort wall, and this may mask the site of the west gate. Certainly the camber of a Roman road is visible today in the field 100 m. west of the fort, and it appears to be heading for the chapel, which may well therefore occupy the site of the main gate. In the absence of excavation however this must remain speculation. If the chapel does not over-lie a gate, however, it may rest on a projecting bastion. Semi-circular, solid bastions projected from the corners of the fort, and Mr. Hull has produced good evidence for the existence of similar ones at intervals of approximately 33 m. all along the western wall; the chapel coincided with the estimated position of one of these.

Very little excavation of any description has been carried out on the site. In 1865 some trenches were cut in the interior but yielded no sign of any structures. In view of the very insubstantial nature of the internal buildings recently uncovered inside Portchester Castle, however, it is quite likely that similar remains were encountered at Bradwell, which the nineteenth-century excavators failed to recognise. The recorded finds from the site include large quantities of Roman pottery and coins, most of it, as is to be expected, of late Roman date.[34]

Whereas some remains at least are still preserved at Bradwell, coastal erosion has now totally removed the other Saxon Shore fort in the canton, that at Walton Castle, Suffolk. We are left completely reliant on records made before the eighteenth century for our knowledge of the site.

Today Walton overlooks three large river estuaries, those of the Orwell, Deben and Stour, which together form the modern harbour of Harwich. It must have been an exceptionally fine position for a fort, though it is possible that in Roman times there was only one river opening to the sea, near Butts Cliffs, Felixstowe, where the fort once stood.

The last remnant of the fort was washed away in the eighteenth century, but we are fortunate in having records made by a local antiquary, Dr. Knight, of the remains surviving in 1722. Knight describes the fort wall as built of stone with bonding courses of tile, 3.6 m. wide, and standing up to 1.5 m. high. This wall ran for 90 m. parallel to the coast before turning sharply at a corner. Unfortunately Knight does not tell us which corner this was, nor do we know whether or not the 100 yards over which the wall ran was the total width of the original fort. Dr. Knight also noted several fragments of buildings, some visible only at low tide, but of these we know virtually nothing, and some at any rate may be associated with the twelfth-century castle which also stood on the site. In addition to Dr. Knight's notes there is in existence a plan and drawing made in 1623. The drawing shows a stone wall with projecting corner bastions, similar to those at Bradwell, but both plan and drawing leave many questions unanswered, and it is quite possible on the basis of them alone that one corner bastion and one interval bastion are represented rather than two corner bastions. Of the date of Walton Castle we know nothing, and it is only on the basis of its plan, so imperfectly known anyway, and its siting, that it is assigned to the Saxon Shore system.[35]

As time went on pressure from Saxon marauders did not decrease, and the coast of the Trinovantian canton, exposed as it was to the attentions of raiders from outside the empire, may have required additional defences. We shall see in chapter 6 how in the later fourth century Germanic mercenaries and *laeti* were brought into the canton to provide extra garrisons, and it is possible that extra lookout posts or signal stations were also added during the fourth century. We mentioned above that the fortlet at Hadleigh may be either first-century, or part of a late Roman defensive system. Only excavation will provide an answer. Concentrations of Roman material at Shoebury, Southminster and Great Wakering may also mask late Roman coastal sites, while north of the Trinovantian-Icenian border the alignment of Roman roads and a number of Roman finds suggest a settlement near Dunwich, probably the *Sitomagus* of the Antonine Itinerary.

Civilian life in the late Roman period

Behind the coastal defences life seems to have progressed placidly enough, and in spite of references to raiding Saxons we cannot as yet point to any site and claim that here we have definite and positive evidence for destruction by hostile forces, Saxon or otherwise.

The Trinovantian canton fell into Britannia Superior when the province was divided into two after the usurpation of Albinus in 197, and into Britannia Maxima after the further subdivision of the province in the early fourth century. During the usurpation of Carausius, 286-93, coins of this British emperor were minted at London and at another mint, marked on the coins as C. This it has been claimed may stand for *Camulodunum*, but *Clausentium* and *Corinium* have equal if not stronger claims. The mint was closed after the overthrow of Allectus in 296. Colchester however probably retained considerable prestige both as the province's oldest *colonia* and as the original capital.

Assumptions of the prestige of Colchester have led to suggestions concerning the three British bishops who attended the Council of Arles in 314, called to debate the Donatist schism. The council was attended by five British representatives, including Eborius, bishop of York, Restitutus from '*civitate Londiniensi*' and Adelphius from '*civitate colonia Londiniensium*'. Unfortunately the surviving text is corrupt and the copyist has become confused by the similarity of the names Lincoln and London; it is probable that Adelphius came from London, which had almost certainly achieved the status of a *colonia* by the fourth century, and Restitutus from Lincoln, although the opposite could be true. The three bishops were accompanied by a deacon and a priest, and it is likely that the five representatives came from the capital towns of the four provinces into which early fourth century Britain was divided; for some reason the fourth capital, *Corinium*, sent no bishop; he may have been too old or ill to attend and been represented by the priest and deacon instead. An alternative theory, however, is that '*colonia Londiniensium*' is a corruption of *colonia Camulodunensium* and that Adelphius was the senior bishop, attended by two assistants or secretaries, the priest and the deacon. This theory would make Colchester the religious centre for Britain as a whole, where Christianity simply took over the original provincial centre of the imperial cult. The later history of the Temple of Claudius itself is not yet fully understood. Mr. Hebditch's excavations in 1964 on the south front of the temple court showed that it had been maintained in a good state of repair until at least the second half of the fourth century when the blocking walls in the arcade were re-plastered. By this time of course Christianity was not only the official religion of the empire, but was well established in the province. If Colchester continued to be the religious centre it may be more than coincidence that directly overlying the pagan altar in front of the temple are the remains of a small apsidal pre-Norman chapel, dedicated to St. Helena, mother of Constantine.

Certainly Christianity was flourishing among the Trinovantes in the fourth century. From Brentwood comes a fine gold finger ring, inscribed with the Chi-Rho monogram, while another Chi-Rho symbol, this time of an unusual design, has recently been found scratched on a tile at Wickford.[36] It is also worth noting that at least one of the Romano-Celtic temples at Colchester was deliberately destroyed, in the late fourth century, possibly by militant Christians.

It is perhaps worth mentioning here a curious but persistent tradition, recorded in the Colchester Oath Book in the fourteenth century, and thereafter repeated by later writers, among them Daniel Defoe.[37] It concerns Helena, whom it describes as the daughter of Coel, 'Duke of the Britons', and who was not only born at Colchester herself, but also gave birth to Constantine there. The dates in the account are confused, and the whole episode is clearly at variance with historical facts, but it is possible that Constantine spent some time in Colchester during his stay in Britain and that his association was magnified in local tradition.

The continued prestige of Colchester, if such prestige indeed existed, would not necessarily have had much effect on the Trinovantes, except in so far as a flourishing town will benefit the surrounding area economically. An attempt has been made in this chapter to summarise the political history of the Trinovantes until the mid fourth century. It is necessarily an incomplete and patchy account, as only in the first century did the Trinovantes catch the attention of the contemporary writers whose works have survived, and so only then do we have anything approaching a full political account. In the late Roman period the troubles of this part of Britain again attracted the notice of writers, although no such detailed account has survived. No writer however dealt with the economic or social life of the people themselves, and the changes that they underwent throughout the 400 years of Roman rule. It is the questions raised when we come to look at the Trinovantian farms and settlements and the social and economic organisation of the tribe in the Roman period that the following three chapters will examine.

3.

Communications and Urban Settlement

The two major Roman roads in the territory of the Trinovantes have both been followed very closely by modern routes, the A12 and A120. Little has been seen of them in excavation, but their course seems clear for most of their length (fig. 15). The road from London to the *colonia* and north into the territory of the Iceni is mentioned as part of two routes of the Antonine Itinerary, which records the main stages and distances (in Roman miles) of journeys made through the empire in the third century.[1]

Extracts from Iter V and Iter IX

Iter V			Iter IX		
Londinio (London)			*Venta Icenorum* (Caistor)		
Caesaromago (Chelmsford)	MP XXVIII		*Sitomago* (Dunwich?)	MP XXXII	
Colonia (Colchester)	MP XXIV		*Combretovio* (Coddenham)	MP XXII	
Villa Faustini (Scole)	MP XXXV		*Ad Ansam* (Stratford St. Mary)	MP XV	
Icinos (Caistor)	MP XVIII		*Camoloduno* (Colchester)	MP VI	
			Canonio (Kelvedon)	MP IX	
			Caesaromago (Chelmsford)	MP XII	
			Durolito (?)	MP XVI	
			Lundinio (London)	MP XV	

Most of the places mentioned in these *itinera* are easily identifiable, with the help of the distances given (see below, p. 91). *Durolitum* is the chief exception. It has traditionally been placed at or near Romford (its Celtic name means walled town on a ford); but that site has not produced

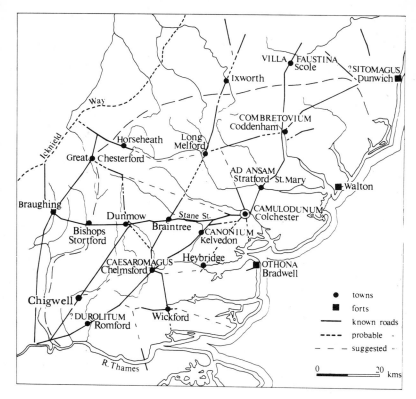

Fig. 15. Roads and urban settlement in the canton

significant quantities of Roman material. On the other hand
recent work on the settlement near Chigwell on the Roding
has suggested that this site might be important enough to
justify the description; this would also provide an explan-
ation for the variation in the distance from London to
Chelmsford between the two *itinera*. The road from London
to Chigwell has recently been excavated, and it remains to be
seen whether this theory will be confirmed by the discovery
of a road linking Chigwell with Chelmsford. No settlement in
this part of the county has yet been shown to have been
walled.[2]

Sightings of the London-Colchester road have generally
been limited to observation of modern road works, apart
from excavations carried out where it passes through settlements, for instance at Chelmsford. The route through

Kelvedon remains obscure, since it has not been found in the
expected place, east of the modern road, during any of the
recent excavations. In London the road was recently uncovered near its crossing of the Lea, south of the modern
route, at Old Ford, confirming Defoe's description of a
causeway in that area. The road left Colchester by the East
gate and followed the line of the modern road to Stratford
St. Mary. Its course from here to Coddenham is less clear, but
it has been excavated south of the settlement. North of
Coddenham it is followed by the modern road to Scole. The
branch from Coddenham to Dunwich given in *Iter IX* can
also be traced along a modern road alignment.[3]

The other major road (Stane Street) followed the existing
Belgic route from *Camulodunum* west to the settlement at
Braughing and thence to *Verulamium*. Here again little
excavation has been done, but the course of the road through
Braintree and Dunmow seems beyond question. Where they
have been seen, both of the major roads were very solidly
metalled with local materials, generally gravel. It is possible
that this metalling was not laid down until at least late in the
first century, since it has been found to overlie late first
century coins and pottery.[4]

Although there is as yet very little evidence, it would seem
that the other roads in the area may have been less solidly
built, although this may simply be the result of greater
weathering in the places where they have been excavated.
The road from London to Chigwell presumably continued
along the line of the modern road and parish boundaries to
Dunmow. Another road chiefly suggested by the modern
alignment is that from Chelmsford to Braintree, with a
branch to Dunmow; piles from a bridge were also found at
Little Waltham. This road, if projected north from Braintree,
runs on through the settlement at Gestingthorpe to Long
Melford. Excavation here has shown it going on towards the
settlement at Ixworth. A road linking Coddenham to Long
Melford can also be traced, and it seems likely that this may
have continued up the Stour Valley to join the road which is
known north of Great Chesterford. From Great Chesterford a
road heading for Colchester is known from air photography,
confirmed by excavation, as far as Radwinter, but cannot be

traced further. Lanes and parish boundaries suggest a turning from this road to Dunmow.[5]

Air photography, fieldwork and excavation in the area of the *colonia* have confirmed the existence of a number of minor roads; south to Mersea, and in the direction of the port at Heybridge, north towards Nayland and Long Melford and north-west up the Colne valley. It is very difficult to tell, however, whether these roads have any more than local significance. The important site at Gosbecks was served by a road branching off the London road at Easthorpe (below, p. 113).[6]

Recent work in south Essex has added considerably to our knowledge of roads in this area.[7] The road from Chelmsford to Great Baddow has been excavated, and parish boundaries continue the line from there to the important site at Wickford, where it has been shown to join an east-west road, which may link with that picked up further west at Billericay. At East Tilbury there was probably a road taking traffic from the ferry which is known to have crossed the Thames here, and a similar road probably linked Wickford with Canvey Island. Another road probably linked Chelmsford with the port at Heybridge and another can be traced from the fort at Bradwell.

New evidence is constantly coming to light to confirm the existence of suspected roads, or to suggest new ones. Doubtless the whole area was covered by a network of minor roads, whose chief function was to provide local transport of goods and produce, rather than long distance communications.

The tribal capital

In Britain, as in other provinces of the Empire, each tribe had its own tribal town, or cantonal capital, imperative for the operation of the Roman system of provincial administration in civilian areas. The cantonal capitals were run by the *ordo*, a council of 100 decurions from whose ranks were drawn the two annual magistrates and their two assistants the *aediles*, who between them were responsible for running the administration during their year in office. The *ordo* was formed from the tribal landowners, initially probably the old Celtic aristocracy, whose members might finance or embellish public buildings in the cantonal capital. The major administrative buildings of the town (forum, basilica and baths) are, however, more likely to have been financed by the whole tribe, perhaps sometimes with additional support from the provincial government, since these were buildings essential to Roman town life.

The system seems to have worked smoothly enough over most of the civilian zone of Britain, but so far, alone among the tribes of southern England, no cantonal capital has been positively identified for the Trinovantes. It may be that in the early phases of the Roman occupation, the ranks of the Trinovantian aristocracy were somewhat depleted after the opposition led first by Caratacus and then Boudicca. Was the lack of a suitable native *ordo* to blame for the apparent absence of the tribal capital? On the other hand, the Roman government would have been quite capable of making up the ranks of the aristocracy with new, pro-Roman, recruits; the Icenian tribal capital was established at Caistor by Norwich in the Flavian period, although admittedly the baths and forum were not built until the middle of the second century.[8]

Major towns are scarce in both Icenian and Trinovantian territory, and although it is possible that there is still a town awaiting discovery,[9] on present evidence Colchester is the only large town in the canton. The situation among the Trinovantes is thus quite different to that which existed among the Coritani and the Dobunni. In the territory of these tribes, first-century *coloniae* were established, but in both cases another highly Romanised town, the cantonal capital, grew up in another part of the canton, Leicester in the case of the Coritani, and Cirencester in that of the Dobunni. Neither Leicester nor Cirencester were less Romanised or prosperous than the *coloniae*, except possibly in their earliest phases. As we shall see, however, the Trinovantes seem to have been unable to produce anything comparable to Colchester in their canton, although a number of small urban settlements are known, and on present evidence Colchester seems to be the most likely location of the tribal administration (fig. 16).

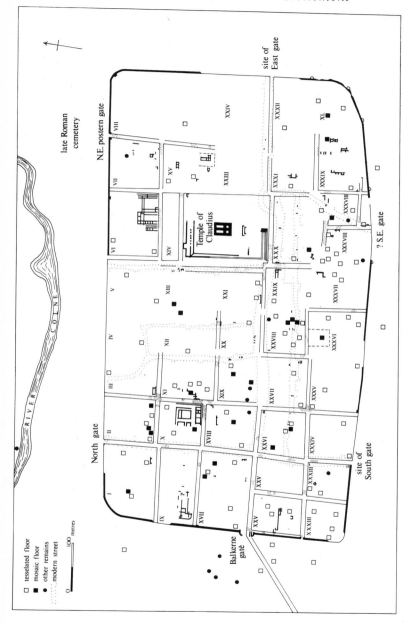

Fig. 16. Roman Colchester

The early history of the town was exceptionally well documented by Tacitus. From his *Annals* we learn that the *colonia* (*Colonia Claudia Victricensis*) was founded in A.D. 49-50, as a town for veteran soldiers, its purpose being both to demonstrate the art of Roman town life, and to act as a garrison for the surrounding, and as yet not entirely subdued, area.[10] From Tacitus we also learn that Colchester was a luxury town, where more attention was paid to amenities than to defence. It was originally intended to be the provincial capital; apart from the *municipium* at *Verulamium* it was the only chartered town in the Claudian period, and it was here that the centre of the imperial cult was established.

The Temple of Claudius, centre of the cult, is undoubtably the most impressive building known to us from the *colonia*. The existence of masonry remains beneath the Norman keep of Colchester Castle (traditionally named King Coel's Palace) has been known for centuries. It was not until 1920, however, that Sir Mortimer Wheeler positively identified the masonry as the remains of a classical temple.[11] Wheeler was able to demonstrate that the castle keep had been built around a pre-existing masonry platform of massive proportions, built over four sand-filled vaults and measuring 24 x 32 m., with foundations sunk 4 m. deep. Wheeler pointed out that such a platform could only be the remains of a large classical *podium*, that is, the raised base on which rested the superstructure of a classical temple. In view of its size, which exceeds that of classical temples normally found in provincial towns, it is now generally agreed that this must be the remains of the Temple of Claudius mentioned by Tacitus, Seneca and Suetonius.

The surviving *podium* is almost certainly the original first-century work, since being fire-proof it would have survived the Boudiccan revolt. Very little, however, is known about the superstructure of this building or of its successor in the post-Boudiccan period.

The upper surface of the *podium* stood over 3 m. above the Roman ground level and must have been approached by a flight of steps in the classical tradition, and indeed the entire superstructure presumably conformed to the classical design of *cella*, peristyle and triangular roof. The upper surface of the *podium* was built of fine white mortar with a bonding course of tile. This probably provided a base for a stone or marble floor, but the original Roman surface was torn out, either in late Roman or in Norman times, and none of the floor remains. The superstructure was doubtless elaborately decorated originally, but again, no trace of this survives.

Just south of the south face of the *podium*, at the base of the hypothetical steps, were remains of a large rectangular altar, surrounded by a vaulted masonry drain and flanked by two large bases, each perhaps for a statue. As suggested in the previous chapter (above, p. 47) it is likely that the altar was the first structure to be built on the site, founded and dedicated during Claudius' lifetime.[12]

The Temple of Claudius stood in a large court occupying (in its final form) 177 x 107 m. and covering the whole of the unusually large *insula* 22. Little is known of any subsidiary buildings in this court in the pre-Boudiccan period, but excavations in 1964 by Mr. Hebditch on its southern side revealed traces of a timber structure apparently predating the fire of 60, and *possibly* linking the Temple court with the pre-Boudiccan building in *insula* 30.[13] So far no other subsidiary buildings are known at this date, and it may be that the pre-Flavian temple stood in an area kept free of any other buildings and specially reserved for an elaborate precinct whose actual construction was delayed by the Boudiccan revolt. On the other hand, it is possible that traces of pre-Boudiccan timber buildings have been destroyed by the massive foundations of the late first century structures.

South of the Temple of Claudius, in the pre-Boudiccan period, were two large buildings of public rather than private character, and although largely built of wattle and daub, they were elaborately decorated with ornate stucco moulding, producing an impressive appearance despite their humble construction. Little is known of the plan of either building, but both were covered by the thick layers of burnt debris that resulted from the Boudiccan sack of the town. The building in *insula* 30 was unfinished at the time of the fire, and it is possible that burnt timber remains and the mortar floor found by Mr. Hebditch on the southern side of the Temple court are part of the same building.[14]

At first it may seem surprising that the Temple of Claudius and the two buildings to the south of it should not occupy the most prominent position, but lie on the eastern edge of the early *colonia*, which was concentrated on the higher ground on North Hill. The situation at Colchester is, however, analogous with that at Lyons, where the altar of the Three Gauls, dedicated to Roma and Augustus, lay outside the town and downhill from it. The Temple of Claudius was associated with the province rather than simply with the *colonia*, which may also explain why it stood on the outskirts of the town, and it is possible that the buildings south of it also had provincial rather than colonial connections.

Tacitus mentions other public buildings in Colchester at the time of the revolt, a theatre and *curia*, and although no definite trace of either has yet been found, it is not unreasonable to expect them in the western part of Colchester, forming part of the Claudian *colonia* that they served. The statue of Victory, however, to which Tacitus also refers, may have stood in the precinct of the Temple of Claudius.[15]

Excavation in the 1960s showed that the Claudian *colonia* may have been somewhat smaller than was once thought, and probably occupied only two thirds of the area later enclosed by the town walls. Distribution of early material (Claudian coins and pre-Flavian samian), and burnt levels attributable to the Boudiccan destruction of the town, occupy the area centred on North Hill, roughly that covered by the earlier fort (fig. 9).[16]

The inhabitants of the early *colonia* enjoyed a comparatively high standard of living, and it is clear that when Tacitus claimed that Colchester was a model town he was being strictly accurate. It is possible that the first colonists occupied pre-existing military structures. At least one military building in *insula* 36 was re-used in the pre-Boudiccan *colonia* and there may have been other examples.[17] The early timber building in *insula* 11 was carefully demolished before the erection of the overlying building, which was later destroyed in the Boudiccan revolt, and similarly the pits associated with military equipment in *insulae* 25 and 10 had been deliberately filled in before the construction of the buildings burnt in 60. Items of military equipment were found in the burnt deposits in both *insulae* 11 and 25 and it is by no means impossible that there was more than one phase of military buildings in Colchester, the latest of which were taken over by the first colonists.

Whatever the initial date of the pre-Boudiccan buildings on North Hill, the standard of building was high. Individual houses were often of complex plan, either built with pebble and mortar dwarf walls, on which rested the superstructure of unbaked clay blocks, or simply wattle and daub. Painted wall plaster and roofing tiles are not uncommon finds in the burnt material which smothers these early buildings, while the storehouse in *insula* 10 boasted at least one mortar floor and was equipped with a piped water supply. The pre-Boudiccan lamp shop in *insula* 11 has already been mentioned, as have the two pottery shops in *insulae* 19 and 28, both of them stocked with expensive pottery and glass imported from south Gaul and the Rhineland. All this speaks of a standard of living that was high even compared to that in contemporary London and *Verulamium*.

The plan of the town in its earliest form is still incompletely known, but even at this early stage the *colonia* must have been densely built up. The distribution of sites that have produced evidence of Boudiccan destruction, is also relevant in this context (fig. 9). It demonstrates clearly how crowded the buildings in the west and centre of the town must have been, since of the sites recently excavated, only one has yielded no evidence of pre-Flavian activity.

A kilometre west of the town, around the Royal Grammar School and West Lodge Road, was a small cemetery, lining the main London road. In later times this was to become an extensive and wealthy burial ground, but early grave groups show that it was already in existence in the pre-Boudiccan period and some of the offerings buried in the mid first-century graves reinforce the impression of good living that has already been noted in the town itself. The impressive sandstone tombstone surmounted by a sphinx, and the famous 'child's grave' with its collection of pipeclay toys or figurines and glazed flagons imported from the Rhineland, are both of Claudio-Neronian date.

This luxury was short lived. Tacitus explicitly states that no defences had been provided, and Mr. Crummy has demonstrated[18] that by A.D. 60 the fort ditch had already been filled in and a north-south street laid over it, while the east-west street between *insulae* 12 and 20 overlay the much compressed remains of a Claudian rampart.[19] Consequently eleven years after its foundation the *colonia* still had no protection against Boudicca and her followers, and the town was completely destroyed in the revolt; the dramatic and widespread evidence of this destruction has already been described in the previous chapter.

Recovery after the revolt was slow and for some years the *colonia* must have remained comparatively small. The plan showing the distribution of pre-Flavian samian and Claudian coins (fig. 9), also reflects conditions after the Claudio-Neronian period, since both categories would continue in use and circulation for some years after their original issue. Of the eighteen sites published in recent years, only one has shown signs of re-building within about five years of the disaster, while in *insula* 10 the extensive storehouse of the pre-Boudiccan period was replaced ten years later by a small workshop, occupying only one corner of the site and surely indicating a change both in use and ownership.[20]

From the Flavian period onwards, rebuilding was in full swing over the North Hill area, where houses were constructed with masonry foundations (albeit with daub superstructures) and not infrequently with mortar floors, painted wall plaster and tiled roofs. The occupation at the east end of the town was, by contrast, of a lower standard. Here the earliest levels usually consist of deposits of sandy clay or loam, with occasional lumps of septaria, plaster or pieces of tile, and sometimes incorporating burnt patches and dark 'occupation' layers. These deposits have been interpreted as the weathered remains of daub and timber buildings.[21] Masonry remains do not appear here much before the second century.

An impressive feature of the post-Boudiccan town is the system of sewers and water pipes with which the *colonia* was provided. Many of the north-south streets, as well as at least two east-west ones, had a fine masonry vaulted sewer running along one side. These sewers stand nearly a metre high with a width of a metre at the base, and are thus large enough for a boy or small adult to crawl along when necessary for cleaning. Small feeder drains led into some of the sewers at intervals, presumably from individual houses, and in places the junction was covered by a manhole and inspection shaft.

Running along at least three of the east-west streets were timber water pipes, joined by iron collars and presumably supplying fresh water to individual houses and possibly to public fountains. It is not yet known how, or from where, the water supply reached Colchester, but a leat or small aqueduct from the Lexden Springs, 2.5 km west of the town, seems likely.[22]

The street grid itself follows two slightly differing alignments. In the western part of the *colonia* the streets are based on the original military layout. However, Mr. Crummy has drawn attention to a slight change in the alignment of the streets in the eastern part of the *colonia*. He suggests that this change probably took place in the pre-Boudiccan period, or possibly in some instances shortly after the revolt, when the streets in the eastern part of the old fortress were re-aligned slightly more to the north and the grid extended east-wards.[23]

The opening years of the second century saw a surge of public building in the town. There is no direct evidence for the rebuilding of the Temple of Claudius itself after the Boudiccan revolt, but it is inconceivable that Roman prestige could have allowed the principal centre of the imperial cult in Britain long to remain in ruins. The Norman keep, however, has removed all trace of the temple's superstructure and with it all record of the temple's history.

Although we may assume a rapid rebuilding of the temple, the magnificent court which surrounded it was not built until the end of the first century. In *c.* 100 a massive *temenos* wall, some 3 m. wide, was erected around the court, an area which seems to have been shifted slightly east of its pre-Boudiccan position so that the temple no longer lay squarely in the centre. On the south side of the court the *temenos* wall was expanded into a massive platform, 4.5 m. wide, on which

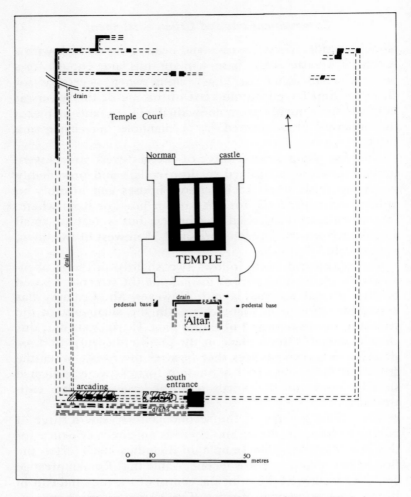

Fig. 17. The Temple of Claudius and its court (after D. Clarke)

stood an arcade of open arches flanking a central gateway of monumental proportions, where fragments of moulded decoration, carved stone, including alabaster, and coloured marble fragments from as far afield as Egypt and Greece have been found. Other buildings, whose character is not yet fully understood, are preserved beneath the Norman rampart on the north side of the temple court, and the whole area was provided with its own elaborate system of drains (fig. 17).[24]

This ambitious and doubtless very expensive work on the

Temple of Claudius is particularly surprising in view of the fact that by 100, when it took place, Colchester had ceased to be the provincial capital. Colchester had been chosen as the capital in 50, but by the time of the Boudiccan revolt the commercial centre was already shifting to London. It was here that the procurator, Catus Decianus, was stationed with his troops when the colonists appealed to him for assistance in 60. By 100 the Provincial Council, which met in the provincial capital, had its headquarters in London, which would lead one to expect the Imperial cult, one of the main concerns of the Provincial Council, to be centred there also. It is therefore not at all certain what role the temple at Colchester now played, although it continued to be a magnificent building, carefully maintained until the late fourth century when the arcade was re-plastered.

South of the Temple of Claudius, the public buildings in *insulae* 29 and 30 were rebuilt, although the date at which this took place is not certain. On both sites large masonry footings, in places over 2 m. wide, were cut through the layer of Boudiccan burnt debris, while those in *insula* 30 were themselves sealed by a second burnt layer, probably dating from the later second century. It is therefore possible that the building in *insula* 30, at any rate, was contemporary with the surge of civic building in the early second century. The plan of both buildings is unfortunately not known, since in the case of the *insula* 29 building only one corner was available for excavation, while all that was seen of the *insula* 30 building were small portions of walling exposed in 1969-70.[25] It may well be that, like its pre-Boudiccan predecessor, this building was also part of the Temple of Claudius complex. The temple court at this period was bounded on the south by an open arcade which would link the two buildings rather than separate them.

Massive masonry walls of early second century date have been found in *insulae* 18, 20 and 31. In *insula* 20 a 2 m. wide masonry wall was built in *c*. A.D. 120 and occupied the central *insula* inside the walled town. In *insula* 31 a substantial building, with walls over a metre wide, was constructed at about the same time, and the inclusion within the building of at least three hypocausts raises the question

whether these could have been the public baths. There is
however no supporting evidence and other sites have claims
at least as strong. Finally in *insula* 18 a massive wall, 1.5 m.
wide, was found in 1965 in an *insula* that occupied a central
position in the fortress and early *colonia*, and which was
served by a large drain.[26] All these massive remains suggest
substantial buildings, although it must be borne in mind that
the hill which the *colonia* occupied was to some extent
terraced in the Roman period and some of these large walls
may have been earth retaining walls.[27]

Among the most costly of all public works must have been
the town defences. After the Boudiccan revolt the town
seems to have been provided with an earthwork defence.
Excavations by Mr. Crummy on the west of the town near the
Balkerne Gate have revealed a defensive ditch, filled in
deliberately at sometime around 80, if not before. In view of
Tacitus' assertion that at the time of the Boudiccan revolt
Colchester had no defences, this ditch may well have been
dug immediately after 60, possibly connecting with an
east-west ditch running on the south side of the town. If this
was the case, it could suggest that much the same area was
enclosed as that occupied by the fortress. In 1964 and
1967 a V-profile ditch, 2.4 m. wide and 1 m. deep, was found
running along the north side of *insulae* 1 and 2, 90 m. inside
the line of the later town wall. The ditch does not seem to
have lain open long before being deliberately filled in. It is
not certain when this infilling took place, but the ditch was
overlain by an early second-century house, and as there was
no sign of intervening occupation it was suggested that the
ditch might be part of a late first-century defence. In the
light of Mr. Crummy's more recent discoveries, it now seems
possible that it belonged to the immediately post-Boudiccan
defensive works, or even to the Claudian fortress.[28]

The Roman town wall still stands for most of its 3.3 km
length. Recent excavations have shown that this wall, unlike
most other town walls of the second and third centuries, was
originally free-standing. The rampart behind it was not
thrown up until some years later, and was largely composed
of domestic refuse or debris from wattle and daub houses
rather than of material derived from the town ditch, as was

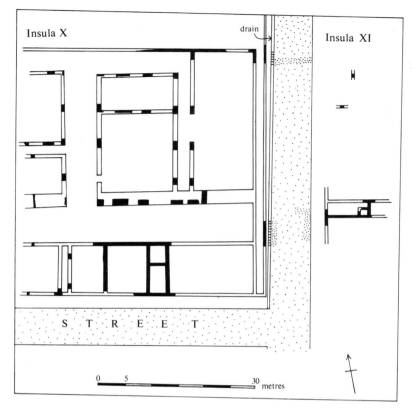

Insula X   drain   Insula XI

S · T · R · E · E · T

0   5   30 metres

Fig. 18. Second-century houses on North Hill, Colchester

usually the case. It is not yet certain when the main ditch in front of the wall was cut.

The date of the town wall has recently been reviewed.[29] It was once thought that it was constructed in the early third century, a date that agreed with that of most town walls in Britain, but it now appears that the Colchester wall may have been built as early as the mid second century, and so be among the earliest stone walls from the province. It was dominated on the west by the Balkerne Gate, through which passed the main road from London.[30] This enormous gate, the largest known from Britain, was a quadruple structure; a double carriage-way and two pedestrian ways were flanked by quadrant-shaped guard rooms. It measured 32.1 m. in width, projected 3 m. from the front of the wall, and was

probably about 12 m. high, thus rising twice the height of the
town wall, which is estimated to have been 6 m. high. The
massive projecting structure, doubtless originally decorated
with mouldings or pilasters, has found no parallel among the
humbler twin towered gates more common from Roman
towns in Britain.

Little is known of the other gates of the *colonia.* The East
Gate was still standing as late as the seventeenth century, but
most of it collapsed in 1651. A sketch by John Constable,
the landscape painter, in 1813 shows part of what may have
been a wing wall of a guard room, which suggests that a large
and elaborate gate, perhaps comparable with the Balkerne
Gate, may once have stood here.

The second century was a prosperous time for the *colonia*,
and by the middle decades extensive private houses, often
with fine mosaics, were not uncommon. Part of one such
house was excavated on North Hill in 1965 (fig. 18) and
consisted of two ranges of rooms connected by corridors.
The southern range may well have been the principal
residential wing of the house, for three of the six rooms
excavated here produced polychrome mosaics (figs. 19-21).
The remaining rooms had plain tessellated floors. To the
north of the building there appears to have been a courtyard.

There is growing evidence for a fire in the later part of the
second century, which may prove to have destroyed a
substantial part of this flourishing town. A timber building in
insula 17 was destroyed by fire in the Antonine period, and
extensive burnt levels on an adjacent site may be of the same
date.[31] At the other end of the town in *insula* 38 a
tessellated pavement, not earlier than the third century in
date, was found directly overlying the remains of burnt
wattle-and-daub buildings. Further burnt levels sealing
masonry remains have been recorded in *insulae* 29 and 30,
which may also prove to be associated with the same
destruction. These deposits, however, have not been securely
dated, and may even be post-Roman. There is certainly no
proof yet that all these different burnt layers were connected
with each other, nor is it clear how the fires were caused.
Although many of the private houses had stone foundations
in the later *colonia*, the superstructures were often of wattle

Fig. 19. Second-century mosaic from North Hill, Colchester

Fig. 20. Second-century mosaic from North Hill, Colchester

and daub, so accidental fires must always have constituted a grave hazard.

It is clear, however, that the court around the Temple of Claudius had to undergo an extensive refurbishing operation in the late second or third century. The arcade along the south side of the court was now blocked up and new drains were laid on the south and west side, the bases of which were levelled with hundreds of fragments of broken marble sheathing, some showing signs of burning and all clearly re-used material.[32] It is tempting to associate the blocking of the arcade with the destruction of the massive masonry building to the south, in *insula* 30, which was never re-built after a fire. It has already been pointed out that the *insula* 30 building may have been associated with the temple with an open arcade between the two. If this was indeed the case, when the *insula* 30 building was destroyed, the arcade might no longer have been necessary and was consequently blocked in. Unfortunately our evidence about the *insula* 30 building is not at all reliable, based as it is on glimpses seen at different times in a few stanchion holes on commercial sites, so that it is not even certain whether this building was destroyed in the late second century, or substantially later.

Colchester suffers peculiarly and drastically from the absence of late Roman and Mediaeval levels. Hence the historically vital fourth to seventh centuries are only thinly represented. It is certain that the town remained a rich and important centre in the late Roman period. Although late Roman levels are rare, they sometimes survive, particularly in the southern part of the town, and in some places along the High Street, where they have been protected by overlying buildings. On North Hill however, an area where much excavation took place in the 1960s, centuries of fruit growing and gardening have meant that many third and fourth century levels have been removed, together with any later remains. South of the modern High Street lies the area where the Mediaeval town was concentrated, and it may be that here more late Roman levels will be found, sealed and protected by overlying Mediaeval deposits. Indeed, excavations in 1971-2 in *insulae* 28 and 36 have shown that a wealthy house, occupying a large area in *insula* 36, continued

Fig. 21. Second-century mosaic from North Hill, Colchester

in occupation until the end of the fourth century, the site later being occupied by Saxon huts or *grubenhauser*.[33] This sequence may well be found to be repeated in other parts of the town. Even on North Hill, third and fourth-century levels sometimes survive together with bases of a few late Roman rubbish pits dug through them, while hand-made pottery of sixth to seventh-century date has been found in *insulae* 2, 10 and 11.[34] From these as yet meagre deposits it is clear that the town continued to flourish until the late fourth, and probably early fifth centuries, if not later (below, p. 144).

Roman Colchester was not confined within the walls, but was almost completely surrounded by extensive suburbs, cemeteries, temples and industrial sites. Space does not permit a detailed description of these, although the industrial area, covering at least 38 acres, (15 ha.) will be referred to in chapter 5. Of the temples, four lie near the Sheepen site and were doubtless dedicated to native deities, perhaps associated with the earlier occupation on the site. There is some evidence that one temple was deliberately destroyed in the later fourth century, perhaps by militant Christians.[35] Remains of three further temples, including that at Gosbecks, have been found, while dedications to the Sulevian mothers and Mars Medocius Campenses suggest that more await discovery.[36]

Chelmsford (Caesaromagus)

Roman remains at Chelmsford have been known for nearly 200 years, and, excluding cemeteries south-west of the town, cover an area of approximately 22 acres (9 ha.). Until recently little was known about the settlement, but 1969 saw the start of a programme of excavations under the direction of Mr. Drury for the Chelmsford Excavation Committee, which has greatly added to our knowledge of the town.[37]

The Roman settlement lies on the south bank of the river Can, a short distance south-west of the centre of the mediaeval town. The northern edge of the area is low-lying and even today liable to flooding, which makes it at first sight surprising that this apparently unattractive site was chosen for the settlement, in preference to the higher and better drained ground nearby. The answer probably lies in the river-crossing here of the London to Colchester road, especially as the river may well have been navigable up to this point in Roman times (fig. 22).

The Roman name for Chelmsford was almost certainly *Caesaromagus*, meaning the plain or market-place of Caesar. The place is mentioned in the Antonine Itinerary, the Peutinger table and the Ravenna Cosmography. *Iter V* of the Antonine Itinerary tells us that it lies 28 Roman miles from London and 24 from Colchester, and *Iter IX*, 31 Roman miles from London and 21 from Colchester. In fact Chelmsford lies 32 Roman miles from London and 23 from Colchester, and thus it could well be the site of *Caesaromagus*, since minor discrepancies of a few miles are not at all uncommon in the Itinerary.[38] The name *Caesaromagus* is apparently unique in Britain in that it is the only one known to contain the imperial prefix, Caesar, although this is not so uncommon in Gaul. There, however, the prefix was generally bestowed on a new foundation, usually although not invariably intended as a cantonal capital. We do not of course yet know for certain where the tribal capital of the Trinovantes was and at first sight *Caesaromagus* appears a likely candidate. However, the numerous Roman sites which have come to light in the town in recent years, both during the course of commercial excavations and planned scientific work, make it clear that Chelmsford did not fall into the same category of urban settlements as do cantonal capitals. Whatever the original intention may have been, the town never developed into the thriving city which one would expect at the seat of tribal administration. Perhaps in the period immediately after the conquest Chelmsford was designated as the site of the new cantonal capital, but the scheme was later dropped, perhaps after the Boudiccan revolt. Mr. Drury has pointed out that the presence here of a pre-Flavian bath suite would support such a theory. Mr. C.E. Stevens has argued a case for the name having been given to the town in the later Roman period. He has drawn attention to the practice in the late empire as a whole for the sub-division of tribal territories and the establishment of secondary tribal centres for these smaller areas. Stevens suggested that *Caesaromagus* was chosen as the centre for a southern division of the canton, and given the imperial prefix at the same time.[39]

Belgic remains are not uncommon in the vicinity of Chelmsford, but as yet no Belgic occupation has been found in the town itself. There was certainly a fort here in the post-conquest period; occasional finds of military equipment have been recorded from the town and recently two distinct military sites have been pinpointed.

In the area between the river Can and the line that was later taken by the Heybridge road, a military compound was established in the Claudian period, but little is yet known either of its character or history (fig. 22). On the slightly higher ground to the south the existence of a second site, in this case probably a fort, is indicated by a ditch of military type on the east side of the London road. This ditch was cut in the later Claudian period, but did not remain open long before it was deliberately back-filled and timber strip buildings were laid across it.

It is becoming increasingly clear that a settlement was established at Chelmsford before the Boudiccan revolt. Mr. Drury has shown that the circular masonry *laconicum* (heated room in a suite of baths), first recorded in 1849, dates from the pre-Boudiccan period; the *laconicum* was sealed by a burnt layer which contained pre-Flavian samian, so it is likely that the bath building was burnt down at the time of the Boudiccan revolt.

After the revolt, Chelmsford was once again provided with a garrison. The strip buildings overlying the earlier military ditch were dismantled and a new defence erected, which continued in use until *c.* 75-80, when the site was again carefully levelled. In the late first and early second century the town expanded. Rectangular timber strip houses were carefully aligned with their broad sides fronting onto the road, which in time became densely built up, with ribbon development flanking both sides. The houses usually consisted of three rooms served by a passage on one side, and were invariably timber-built, although in the late Roman period the walls often rested on sills of flint and mortar. Roofs were generally thatched, while floors were of gravel or

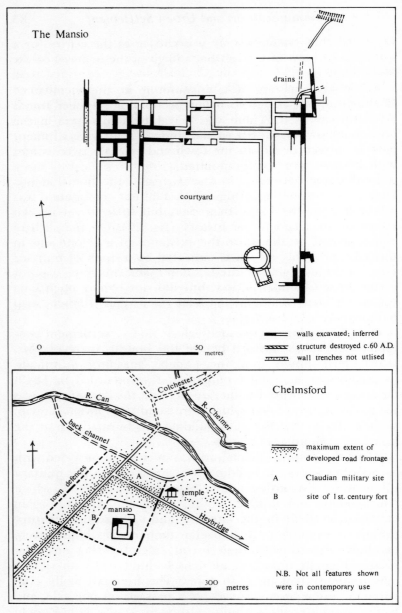

Fig. 22. Plan of Chelmsford and its *mansio* (after Drury)

earth, or on occasion were probably planked.

Roads in Chelmsford seem to have been confined to the main London road and the Chelmsford to Heybridge road which was first discovered by Mr. Drury and has since been sectioned at several points. Apart from these no other streets are known and it is unlikely that Chelmsford ever had a regular lay-out of streets in the grid characteristic of major Roman towns. Ribbon development along the two roads, with perhaps more or less haphazard paths connecting more isolated houses, seems to be the pattern for Roman Chelmsford.

The largest building so far found in Chelmsford is the *mansio*, originally built in timber in the late first century, and subsequently re-built in stone on the same plan in the early second century (fig. 22). The *mansio* was basically a courtyard house, 66 m. square, with an imposing entrance in the north wing added in the third century. The baths lay in the north-east corner and replaced the earlier pre-Boudiccan bath suite of which the *laconicum* was a part.

On the north-east side of the settlement a Romano-Celtic temple was excavated in 1970-1.[40] It occupied a site with a long tradition of sanctity reaching back to the pre-Roman period. In the mid first century A.D. the site was surrounded by a bank and ditch which was replaced later in the century by a complex of timber structures. In *c.* 320 a masonry temple of polygonal plan was erected with an unusual apse to house the cult object. An elaborate entrance porch was added later. This building continued in use throughout the fourth century and into the early fifth, when, after a period of occupation by squatters, the temple was carefully demolished.

Industry in Chelmsford is represented by late Roman pottery kilns and a small smithy excavated south of the town by the Chelmsford Museum in 1965. The overall impression is one of small workshops catering for the needs of the local population, rather than of industry on a large scale. Mr. Drury has suggested that wharves may have existed on the banks of the river Can, a tributary of the Chelmer, and trade is likely to have played a large part in the economy of Roman Chelmsford.

In 1972 a rampart and ditch was excavated by Mr. Drury, which, together with earlier discoveries and observations, suggest that in the late second century an area of 18 acres (7 ha.) was enclosed by a substantial earthwork defence. This defence was used only for a short time before being filled in, but the filling of the ditch contained much burnt debris suggesting a large-scale fire in the town in the late second century, while several sites within the defended area show signs of burning at this time. It is becoming clear that at Chelmsford we have another example of the widespread burning recorded on a growing number of sites in the south and central parts of the canton in the later second century.

In summary, the evidence at present available suggests that Chelmsford falls into the class of small town studied recently by Mr. Todd;[41] a trading and industrial settlement which catered for the rural population of this part of the canton. As in the case of the other small towns of this type, there is little sign of public building apart from the temple, and none of civic planning.

Great Chesterford

Apart from Colchester, Great Chesterford is the only walled town so far located in the canton. One might expect it therefore to have been a place of some importance in the Roman period. Observations made by John Neville in the last century, excavation by Major Brinson in 1948 and aerial photography combine to make up our knowledge of the site.[42] Great Chesterford lies in an area that was already important in the Belgic period, and at the junction of Roman roads from Colchester, Braughing and Cambridge, so it is not surprising to find evidence of considerable Roman occupation. A large quantity of Belgic material has been recovered from Great Chesterford, much of it from deep pits and shafts reminiscent of those excavated more recently at Sheepen, and perhaps with ritual significance.

The military importance of Great Chesterford has long been appreciated, and recently Mr. Rodwell has published evidence for the existence here of a large fort of about 35 acres (14 ha.), capable of accommodating half a legion as well as some auxiliary troops.[4][3] In 1948-9 Major Brinson excavated a section of the ditch on the north-west side of the fort and suggested that it dated from the Neronian period, in which case it probably formed part of the post Boudiccan settlement of the area. No contemporary structures have been excavated within the fort.

It is probable that the civilian settlement, centred around the south gate of the fort, started its life as an extra-mural settlement and that by the second century civilian buildings were standing inside the line of the later town walls. No complete plans of timber buildings have been published, but Major Brinson reports traces of numerous wooden houses of rectangular plan and with gravel or earthen floors, all over the northern sector of the walled area. One at least of these, a timber structure underlying a later masonry building, may date from the early second century or even earlier. Nevertheless the general impression is that the buildings at Great Chesterford were on the whole more substantial than any so far excavated at Chelmsford, with the obvious exception of the *mansio*. Not least indicative of this is the discovery of roller-stamped daub, implying walls coated with plaster and probably painted. Among the earliest dated structures from the town is a small rectangular building of second-century date, which rested on narrow masonry foundations, although the superstructure was probably daub and timber. This building had been rebuilt in the late third or early fourth century. The plan of this new building was that of a corridor villa of the type generally found only in rural contexts, with a hypocaust in one room and a tessellated floor in another. A second masonry building 15 m. to the south was also dated to the fourth century, although apparently from a later phase. Although its plan was simple, a mere two rooms with one opening from the other, among the fallen rubble from the superstructure was part of a stone corniced architrave, which indicates a comparatively superior exterior to this otherwise modest building.

Another imposing structure in the settlement is suggested by a large octagonal block of carved sandstone, discovered in the eighteenth century and now housed in the British Museum. Of the original eight faces only four survive, but on

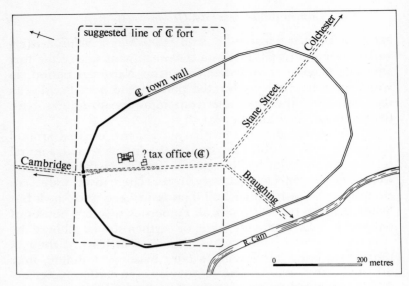

Fig. 23. Plan of Great Chesterford (after Brinson)

each of these are the heads and shoulders of Roman divinities, Mercury, Jupiter, Mars and Venus, all carved in low relief. It is likely that the remaining four faces also bore representations of gods or goddesses. Although ambitious in conception, it is somewhat crudely carved and is clearly provincial work. An attractive suggestion has been made that it is all that remains of a Jupiter column.

In spite of these remains of late Roman date, the settlement seems always to have retained a rather haphazard character (fig. 23). There is no sign that a regular street grid was ever laid out and Major Brinson has described the fourth century town thus: 'Excavation of the northern part of Great Chesterford shows that the tone of the place was essentially rustic and native. The objects of everyday use and the general finish of the buildings follow indeed the simple standards general in remoter provincial districts, but the contrast between this and urban conditions is marked.'[44]

It is consequently surprising to find this small and modest settlement provided with stout defensive walls enclosing a total area of about 36 acres (15 ha.). The walls were still partly standing as late as the eighteenth century, when they were described by Stukeley. Even at that time, however, they were constantly being robbed to provide stone for building and road repair, and today all that remains is a large robber trench. Major Brinson's excavations demonstrated that the walls were built not earlier than the early fourth century; a date near the middle of the century is now generally favoured (below, p. 137).

Other minor urban settlements

Little is known of the remaining small towns in the canton, Braintree, Coddenham, Great Dunmow, Heybridge, Horse-heath, Kelvedon, Long Melford, Romford, Bishop's Stortford and Stratford St. Mary. Some certainly had their origins in the Belgic period. Belgic pottery, sometimes in large quantities, has been collected at Braintree, Kelvedon, Hey-bridge, Coddenham and Long Melford. This was apparently associated with pits and ditches at Braintree and Kelvedon, while at Heybridge, excavations by Mr. Drury in 1972 revealed a strongly defended Belgic site surrounded by a rampart and ditch with an impressive timber gateway. These defences however were never completed and had been deliberately demolished early in the conquest period.[45]

Many of these minor settlements may prove to have superseded earlier forts. Great Dunmow, Braintree and Long Melford occupy route centres, all obvious positions for early military posts, as is Coddenham, where pits containing Claudio-Neronian pottery and a piece of cavalry equipment have been recorded at Baylham Mill. At Kelvedon Mrs. Rodwell has recently recorded a Claudian ditch of military type and several items of military equipment.[46]

Throughout most of their lives these minor settlements display the same comparatively low standard of living as that revealed by the recent excavations at Chelmsford. Nowhere have traces of a regular street grid been found. Mr. Drury, excavating at Great Dunmow in 1970/2, found no sign of either street grid or substantial buildings; instead the exca-vations revealed late Roman stock pens, remains of timber buildings, including a possible shrine of late Roman date, and small boundary ditches, apparently defining individual plots. At Long Melford, however, a black and white tessellated floor has been recorded and other floors and masonry remains have been recorded in the past from the village. Air photographs show part of a masonry building standing in a ditched enclosure. The same settlement has also produced traces of much poorer occupation lining the Roman road for a distance of 1 km.[47]

Excavations by the author at Kelvedon (*Canonium*) in 1968 uncovered two small huts with gravel floors (fig. 24). The western hut dated from the third century and included a tiled hearth set in the centre of a roughly rectangular floor, while the eastern hut, represented only by a worn gravel floor and drainage gully, dated from the late fourth or early fifth century. Traces of similar gravel floors had been found by local people in the surrounding area, but in no case did any trace of superstructure remain; this had probably been of timber, perhaps resting on sills above ground level, but turf work cannot be ruled out entirely. The evidence is thus very incomplete, but a small quantity of slag was found amongst the domestic refuse in the nearby rubbish pits, and the picture that emerges is one of modest workshops, perhaps strung out along the Roman road.

Somewhat similar occupation has since been uncovered by Mrs. Rodwell on the northern side of Kelvedon, as well as a large rectangular building and a circular timber building, which she has interpreted as a temple. This had been burnt down in the late second century, but nearby pits produced a fine lead curse or *defixio* and several letters cut out of sheet bronze. These finds were doubtless associated with the temple.[48]

The remains so far excavated from Kelvedon are thus very similar to those known from Chelmsford, although it is possible that more substantial buildings await discovery. Worn *tesserae* with mortar still adhering to one face and clearly re-used material from a broken up tessellated pavement were found incorporated in the floor of the eastern hut excavated in 1968. Obviously much work remains to be done at Kelvedon, especially in view of the discovery many years ago of pagan Saxon remains in the adjacent parishes of Feering and Inworth.

The evidence of metal working at Kelvedon has just been

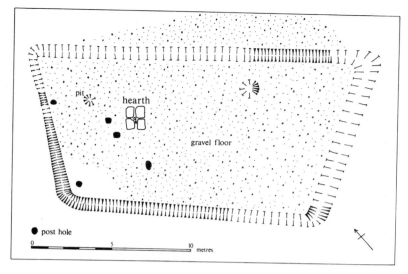

Fig. 24. A third-century hut at Kelvedon

mentioned, but it was doubtless widespread in the smaller settlements. At Heybridge iron slag and lead from casting have been noted by Mr. Drury on a site bordering the river Blackwater. The size of these minor settlements probably varied, but most seem to have been between about 15 and 20 acres (6-8 ha.). Many simply consisted of ribbon development along a main road and gradually tailed off into the countryside. At Great Dunmow Mr. Drury found that individual plots had been delimited by boundary ditches, and while the road frontage was built over, the area behind the houses was given up to stock pens, rubbish pits and doubtless also to vegetable gardens.

Three minor settlements are mentioned in the Antonine Itinerary, *Durolitum, Canonium*, and *Ad Ansam. Canonium*, listed in *Iter IX* as 9 Roman miles from Colchester and 12 from Chelmsford, fits well with Kelvedon (10 miles from Colchester and 12 from Chelmsford) which has already been mentioned. *Ad Ansam*, a Latin name meaning 'at the loop' and presumably referring to a bend in a river, has been identified as Stratford St. Mary, 9.5 km. (6 miles) north-east of Colchester, which fits the mileage quoted in *Iter IX* of the Itinerary (6 miles) very well. Stratford St. Mary lies on the

river Stour, close to the point at which the river must have
been crossed by the Colchester to Caistor-by-Norwich road.
The actual crossing place has not yet been located, although
the general area is known. A few Roman finds have been
recorded from the north bank of the river[49] as well as
evidence of a wealthy villa or estate centre at Capel St.
Mary, 4 km. to the north-east. There is no sign of a
settlement which would warrant the description of even a
minor town, however, so these remains have consequently
been included on the map of rural settlement. As for
Durolitum, we have earlier suggested (above, p. 60) that it
might be identified with the settlement near Chigwell on the
Roding, or with Romford.

Conclusions

A feature that emerges clearly from this survey of the urban
settlements in the canton is the pre-eminent position
occupied by Colchester. Although more substantial buildings
probably await discovery at Chelmsford and Kelvedon and
doubtless also at other settlements, Colchester alone seems to
have been equipped with public buildings and a proper street
grid. It is difficult to see any of the minor settlements as
centres for the tribal administration, and on present evidence
it appears that the tribal capital must have lain at Colchester.
Tacitus mentions native *incolae* apparently living in Colchester before the Boudiccan revolt and it has been suggested
that from its foundation Colchester was intended to provide
the seat of the tribal institutions, although perhaps in a
subsidiary role to those of the *colonia*.[50]

What then was the status of the other settlements? They
all seem to fall into the class of small town recently studied
by Mr. Todd; that is, small centres providing local market
centres for the surrounding rural districts, with modest
workshops supplying goods which were not produced on the
farmsteads in the neighbourhood. It is extremely difficult to
draw the line between small 'towns' like Braintree, Great
Dunmow, and Long Melford, and sprawling 'rural settlements' like Wickford, Gestingthorpe or East Tilbury (below,
p. 119). It may be that settlements at obvious route centres

should be classed as minor towns where officials of the central or provincial administration could be based, while those in more isolated positions, for instance Gestingthorpe, will turn out to be settlements of workers employed on a nearby villa.[51] In the absence of excavation this must remain speculation, and until further research is carried out the distinction between the two types of settlement will remain blurred.

Whatever the status of these settlements, it is certain that there were a considerable number of them, all apparently thriving right down to the very end of the Roman period and in some cases beyond. Although they never seem to achieve more than a very modest standard of Romanisation they nevertheless indicate a prosperous and settled countryside, and as such have an important bearing on the economy of the canton.

4.

Rural Settlement

Our discussion of rural settlement is made extremely difficult by the fact that no villa, nor indeed any rural settlement in the canton, has been totally excavated. Not only do we have no complete villa plans, but all too often the plans which have been recovered are based on unsatisfactory nineteenth-century excavations. Of the fields and farm buildings which were associated with, and were indeed an integral part of, these villas, we know even less.

Much of our evidence for villas rests on nothing more than collections of pottery and building debris picked up by local archaeologists during field work. In this chapter a site will be classed as a probable villa if it has produced not only pottery but also pieces of flue tile and other evidence such as painted wall plaster and remains of tessellated floors. Masonry foundations however have not been considered to be manda-tory in an area where wood and clay are abundant, but stone largely absent. With the exception of septaria, all building stone would have to be imported from a considerable distance, presumably at some expense. For this reason many villas may have been largely, if not entirely, timber built.

The villas

A striking feature of rural settlement in the canton is the concentration of villas in north Essex and south Suffolk; as can be seen from the distribution map (fig. 25), this concentration was particularly dense in the lower Colne valley.[1] A detailed consideration of the villas in this area will

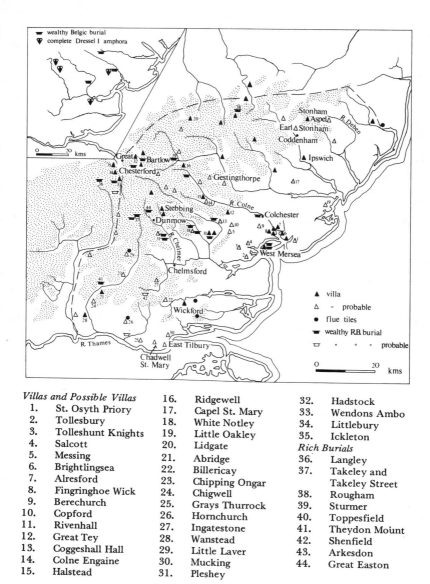

Fig. 25. Wealthy rural settlement in the canton

demonstrate the incompleteness of the evidence at our disposal and the problems that this poses.

On Mersea Island, in the Colne estuary, there was at least one villa, and probably two. Neither has been excavated, but

Fig. 26. Part of a mosaic floor from the villa at West Mersea Church

mosaic floors have been encountered during grave-digging in the churchyard (fig. 26). A tessellated pavement and fragments of painted wall plaster, 60 m. south-west of the church, may lie in another wing of the same, very extensive, house, but mortar and Roman pottery found north of the church must have belonged to a second building of which nothing more is known.[2] It is probable that at least one villa lies at St. Osyth Priory, where first and second century pottery has been recovered and a tessellated floor recorded.[3] South of the Colne, probable villas have been recorded at Tollesbury and Tolleshunt Knights, while walls have been reported from Salcott and Messing which may mark the sites of two further examples.[4]

On the north bank of the Colne, two villas are known at Brightlingsea[5] and in 1885 a substantial winged corridor villa was discovered at Alresford Lodge (fig. 27). The southern corridor was tessellated and the original report mentions numerous pieces of painted wall plaster, some showing three successive coats of paint. Just 11 m. south-west of the main villa was a detached block of five rooms, with the remains of a hypocaust in one of them. This may have been a separate bath block, and it is possible that this is the origin of two flue tiles of Ashtead type, with stamped designs on them typical of the Flavian period. The main villa possibly replaced a timber predecessor contemporary with the bath block, but whatever the case, the presence of the Flavian flue tiles suggests the possibility of a comfortable residence here before the end of the first century, although it must always be remembered that the tiles could have been re-used much later than the date of their original manufacture.[6]

Fingringhoe Wick, overlooking the Colne estuary, was obviously a place of importance in the early Roman period. The site has been extensively quarried for gravel and much has been lost; indeed the site has now been almost completely destroyed, but remains of three separate Roman houses have been recorded. Although none of them has been closely dated, it is clear that all three belonged to the early Roman period. Among the vast quantity of Roman material collected from the site, very few items are of third or fourth century date, while the bulk belongs to the mid first to early second centuries; there is comparatively little material dating after *c.* 120.[7]

There is a possible villa site on the outskirts of modern Colchester at Park Farm, Berechurch, on the south bank of the Roman river, where large quantities of occupation material have been collected, including roof tiles and fragments of painted plaster. The pottery from the site is mainly of first and second century date, although there is a small proportion of third and fourth-century material.[8] A rather similar spread of material has been recorded from fields at Copford, 6 km. west of Colchester,[9] while at Great Tey local archaeologists have partly uncovered a house with tessellated floors and marble veneered walls, which was founded in the later first century.[10] Further west still, debris collected in fields at Coggeshall Hall and Colne Engaine[11] suggests further villas here, while at Halstead, on a north-facing slope

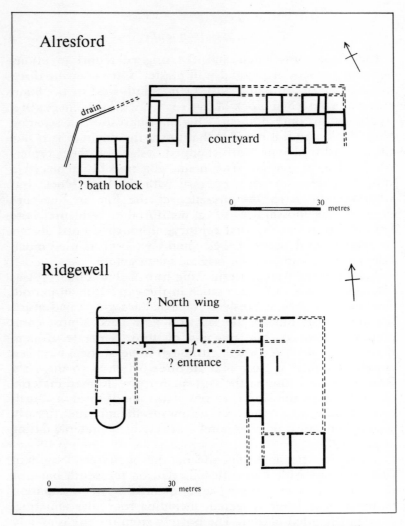

Fig. 27. The villas at Alresford and Ridgewell (after Hull)

overlooking the Colne 20 km. upstream from Colchester, a hypocaust, tesserae and fragments of masonry have been recovered, surrounded by a very extensive area of occupation debris dating from Belgic to later Roman times.[12] Finally at Rivenhall, 20 km. south-west of Colchester, wealthy Belgic occupation was succeeded by two substantial villas, both established by the Flavian period.

All the sites so far described lie within 20 km. of the *colonia.* It is particularly interesting to note that although only seven of the twenty-one sites have seen any sort of excavation, all these excavated examples may well have been founded in the later first, or very early second century.

Turning to the undulating country which forms the block of land between the river Deben and the Icknield way on the one side, and the river Chelmer and the sea on the other, we find that it was liberally studded with villas. Space does not permit detailed descriptions of them all, but an apparently early example was excavated in 1794 at Ridgewell (fig. 27)[13]. The masonry foundations of three wings of the building were uncovered, but the plan shows a small passage in the middle of the central wing, which may have led to more important rooms that were not excavated. In the east wing rooms were found with mortar floors and painted walls, including a small bath suite. Finds from the site include pottery ranging from the mid first century to the fourth century. Some other villas in the area may have started life as early as the first century. Pottery from suspected villa sites at Gestingthorpe, Capel St. Mary, White Notley and Little Oakley covers the entire Roman period and includes first century material. Only excavation will show whether or not a villa existed on any of these sites in the first century. Recent air photographs have revealed a fine corridor villa at Lidgate (fig. 28) on the northern borders of the territory of the Trinovantes, 14 km. south-west of Bury St. Edmunds. The villa is set in what appears to be a ditched enclosure, within which also lies a large rectangular building with external buttresses, possibly a granary. In the absence of excavation the date of the site is unknown.

South of Chelmsford, villas are rarer than further north, as the distribution map (fig. 25) shows. Here again much of the land is clay, in this case heavy London Clay, which as late as the eleventh century was still largely cloaked by dense forest. Roman settlement was by no means uncommon in this area, however, and clearly the forest was extensively nibbled into during the Roman period. Nevertheless, villas appear to be scarce compared with their distribution in the north of the canton. Villas are known or suspected at Abridge, Billericay,

Fig. 28. Aerial photograph of Lidgate villa, with enclosure and but-
tressed granary

Chadwell St. Mary, Chipping Ongar, Chigwell, Grays Thurrock, Hornchurch, Ingatestone, Little Laver, Mucking,
Pleshey, Thundersley, East Tilbury, Wanstead and Wickford.[14]

Many of the villas lie on gravel, either on terraces
overlooking the Thames or on beds exposed in river valleys.
The scattering of villas along the north bank of the Thames
calls for particular comment; it is probable that the influence
of the provincial capital at London, together with the trading
opportunities provided by the Thames, influenced their siting
here as much as the presence of gravel terraces (below, p. 121).
The general tendency of villas to prefer these lighter soils
roughly follows the earlier pattern of Belgic settlement in the
river valleys, although the distribution of Romano-British
settlement as a whole is more widespread. Most of the larger
settlements either have continuity of occupation or else
appear to take over from important Belgic sites within a few
kilometres.

As elsewhere in Roman Britain, villas tend to concentrate around urban centres. Thus Colchester is the focus of the large group in the lower Colne valley, while the small towns each have their own cluster of satellite villas. The Hadstock/ Bartlow group of villas, Wendons Ambo, Littlebury and Ickleton, are all within a radius of 10 km. of Great Chesterford, while the villas at Earl Stonham, Stonham Aspel and Ipswich lie within the same distance of *Combretovium*. Further south, the villas at Stebbing and little Dunmow lie within 5 km. of Great Dunmow while those at Abridge, Wanstead and Hornchurch are within 10 km. of Romford. Chelmsford, surprisingly, has so far no villas in its immediate hinterland except for possible examples, 10 km. from the town, at Ingatestone and Pleshey. This dearth, however, may well be an accident of discovery, which further fieldwork will rectify. Kelvedon on the other hand is within 5 km. of Rivenhall, and Braintree is a similar distance from White Notley, where fragments of painted wall plaster and flue tiles have been recorded.[15]

Wealthy rural burials

There is a concentration of villas in north Essex and south Suffolk which coincides with the distribution of wealthy Romano-British graves (fig. 25). The area centred on the valleys of the Colne and Chelmer, and the upper reaches of the Stour and the Cam, has produced a number of rich burials, known for many years and commented on by the late Professor Richmond.[16] These wealthy graves have their origin in the later Iron Age; the burials at Lexden, Welwyn and Mount Bures have already been described. The tradition however persisted into the early Roman period.

Perhaps the most famous of the wealthy Roman burials is the group of seven (originally eight) *tumuli* at Ashdon in north-west Essex, known locally as the Bartlow Hills. Three of these *tumuli*, on the west of the group, were destroyed in 1832 but all seven were excavated by a local antiquary, John Gage, between 1832 and 1834 and all produced rich grave goods. It has been suggested that the contents of *tumulus* 4 had specific religious associations, since here were found a bronze flagon with silver inlay, a bronze *patera* and ewer and two bronze strigils as well as glass ware and an *amphora*. The base of the flagon was too small to enable the vessel to stand upright and it has been suggested that it was used only during sacrifices, while the strigils have been seen as objects used for ritual cleansing. This in turn has led to the suggestion that the aristocratic family whose members were buried in the Bartlow Hills held the office of High Priest in the Temple of Claudius at Colchester.[17]

Apart from their possible religious significance (a suggestion based on the most tenuous evidence), the Bartlow Hills are by no means unique in the canton. At Rougham, on the northern boundary of the canton, four *tumuli*, arranged in a straight line, were excavated in the last century. Two were found to contain Antonine pottery, including samian, while one produced an interment in a lead coffin, presumably of late Roman date. The Rougham *tumuli* must also be a family cemetery, and traces of what appears to have been a villa were recorded in the nineteenth century '250 yards south of the *tumuli*'.[18] Perhaps this was the family seat. On Mersea Island in the Colne estuary an impressive *tumulus* over 6 m. high overlooks the causeway which, at low water, connects the island with the mainland. When the *tumulus* was excavated in 1912 a small tile-built cist, 81 cm. square, was found. The cist contained a cremation held in a glass urn and accompanied by samian and other pottery of late first-century date. Although the contents were comparatively unpretentious, the task of constructing the *tumulus* can only have been undertaken in honour of an influential and wealthy man. Two km. south-west of the *tumulus*, near West Mersea church, the foundation of a walled burial mound was found in the last century. Although nothing of the super-structure remained it is clear that a mound nearly 20 m. in diameter had been revetted with a masonry wall, relieved by twelve external buttresses. The stress caused by the earthern mound on the wall was taken up by six internal radial walls, producing the 'cartwheel' plan characteristic of such monuments. The date of the tomb unfortunately is unknown, but nearby a small masonry tomb was discovered in 1923. This contained the ashes of a young child and dated from the early second century; it well may be that a wealthy family cemetery lay here, perhaps connected with the villa adjacent to the church (above, p. 95).[19]

Another *tumulus* was excavated in the nineteenth century at Langley and produced glass and samian, although the details have not survived. In 1855 at Takeley Street, what was described as a small mound was dug into. This was probably the much-ploughed remains of another *tumulus*, as beneath it was found a cremation burial in a glass urn, accompanied by seven fine bronzes as well as glass and samian vessels.

Centuries of ploughing must have destroyed many *tumuli* without trace; it is likely for instance that the bronze ewer and bowl ploughed up in the last century in 'Barrow' field, Rivenhall, came from a now vanished *tumulus*.

Tumulus burial was established in our area before the Roman conquest, but the Rougham *tumuli* remind us that the practice continued throughout the Roman period. It is clear nevertheless that this method of burial was most popular in the first and second centuries, when it was probably the rite used by surviving native aristocratic families. *Tumulus* burial however was not the only choice available to them. At White Notley, a brick-built tomb or *columbarium* was found in 1954. The tomb consisted of a small circular masonry foundation, 2.4 m. in diameter, with a sunken, tile-built central chamber 1.24 m. square. In the sides of the chamber were three small niches where cremation urns could have been accommodated. The tomb had already been robbed by the time it was discovered, and only a small quantity of second century material survived. It is likely that this monument was similar to, but on a smaller scale than, the wheel tomb at West Mersea.

In 1750 at Plesheybury Farm a brick vault with small niches in the walls was uncovered; the niches contained urns with cremated bones. An even earlier discovery was made at Coggeshall in the seventeenth century when an 'arched vault of brick' containing Roman pottery was excavated. Yet another brick vault with Roman pottery was discovered at Great Easton in 1850.

Several rich burials are known where the cremation and

grave goods were deposited in wooden chests. Some of these may once have been covered by *tumuli* which have since been ploughed away, but one at least that was recently discovered at Sheepen had simply been buried in the ground.[20] At Takeley a cremation was accompanied by glass, samian, coins (Domitian and Vespasian) and four small bronze rings. All these had been buried in a wooden chest. More recently a cremation accompanied by glass, samian and lion-headed bronze studs was found in the remains of a wooden chest with an iron hasp at Little Walden.

Further rich rural burials have been recorded at Sturmer, Toppesfield, Black Notley, Pleshey, and Theydon Mount, and there are possible examples at Shenfield, Arkesdon and Rickling. Some of these may have been chest burials, no trace of the wooden chest surviving, while others may once have been covered by a *tumulus*, but it is clear that they all represent the graves of a wealthy and influential class. Rougham 4 and Theydon Mount, which produced an indented thumb beaker, must be late Roman, while the date of Great Easton, Coggeshall, Langley, Plesheybury and Shenfield is uncertain, but the remainder date from not later than the second century, while Pleshey, Toppesfield and Bartlow 1 have been assigned to the first.

The wealthy burials show a marked concentration in northern Essex, a distribution particularly interesting when compared with the distribution of the pre-Roman 'Welwyn' type graves (above, p. 11). This distribution has been seen by Dr. Peacock as marking the heartland of the Trinovantes before the Roman conquest and it is tempting to see the early Romano-British burials both as continuing the pre-Roman tradition, and as marking the estates of the Trinovantian nobility after the conquest. This suggests that the nobility retained at any rate some of their ancestral estates, although it is true that if the ranks of the aristocracy had been much depleted as a result of the stands taken by Caratacus and Boudicca, they could have been re-filled with Roman sympathisers. It has already been pointed out that the distribution of wealthy graves broadly corresponds to the concentration of villas in north Essex and south Suffolk. Many of these were doubtless built by the Romanised descendants of the occupants of the early Roman graves, but so far only in the Colchester region has evidence been forthcoming for the widespread construction of villas as early as the first century. Doubtless the early prosperity of the *colonia* was responsible for a corresponding prosperity in its immediate hinterland.

It is not known how long the northern part of the canton continued to be wealthier than elsewhere. Certainly rich graves became rarer as time went on (with the exception of the Colchester cemeteries), but this may simply reflect changes in fashion. The distribution of late Roman stone and lead coffins, probably also an indication of wealth in counties like Essex and Suffolk where building stone is absent, certainly shows no concentration in the northern part of the canton.

Estates

An interesting feature of the canton is the small number of villas that are known in the close vicinity of large areas of occupation debris, sometimes covering many hectares. A good example is provided by the site at Rivenhall.[21]

The site was first scientifically explored in 1950-2, while extensive excavations are currently being directed by Mr. and Mrs. Rodwell. The site is one of considerable interest. Following rich Belgic occupation two villas were built, both of them with origins in the first century. One lies largely beneath the church and little is known of its plan; the other lies a few metres east of the church. In spite of the incomplete evidence so far at our disposal it is clear that this eastern villa was a large, and by Trinovantian standards very large, building. Indeed the plan published as a result of the 1950 excavations hints at a double courtyard building reminiscent of the late courtyard villas of the Cotswolds. These were probably the centres of large estates with numerous subsidiary buildings, barns, bathsuites and accommodation for farm hands. The villas at Rivenhall however did not make up the entire site; Roman remains cover a total area of approximately 30 acres (12 ha.) and range over four centuries. Clearly not all this large area need necessarily have been occupied at one time, and the occupation material which has been recorded may have been spread further by agricultural activities such as the use of farmyard rubbish tips to manure the land, which would involve a considerable scattering of domestic rubbish over the surrounding fields. Nevertheless, the occupation material is fairly dense on the ground and it is certain that a very large area was actually occupied at one time or another. It is not surprising that Rivenhall has in the past been suggested as the site of *Canonium*.

Mr. Todd has suggested that the Rivenhall villas were the centre of a large estate with farm workers and craftsmen living in the area now covered by the occupation debris. This attractive theory has much to commend it, but only extensive excavation can prove it.[22]

A similar estate may have existed north of Colchester at Gestingthorpe. Here large quantities of Roman material have been found, dating from the mid first century right through to the early fifth, and associated with a large complex of buildings. No organised excavation has been carried out but the farmer, Mr. Cooper, has watched the site and from time to time has himself undertaken small scale excavation. Numerous masonry remains and broken pieces of tessellated and mosaic floors have been noted, together with flue tiles and part of an apsidal building which suggests that a bath block was included on the site. No plan however has yet been published. It is clear from Mr. Cooper's observations that many timber buildings existed here as well as the masonry structures.

There are signs that industry, as well as agriculture, was carried on at Gestingthorpe. Remains of metal working, crucibles and slag are frequently ploughed up, and parts of a mould for casting a fine bronze statue indicate that this metal working was not simply to provide equipment for a self sufficient farm, but luxury goods, doubtless destined for a wider market.[23] Secondary industries such as this would have called for many workers as well as the agricultural labourers required on the farm; it is probable that many of the structures on this extensive site would have been the dwellings of the estate staff, and the site as a whole throws interesting light on the social and economic organisation of the tribe in Roman times.

At Stebbing, 4 km. to the north-east of Great Dunmow, two villa sites are known, one of which, at Porter's Hall, may have been an estate centre. The site covers at least 50 acres (20 ha.), but here again little excavation has so far been carried out.[24] Not much is known of the buildings on the site, but masonry remains appear to be extensive and include a bath suite, while fragments of marble wall veneer have been picked up in the fields. Particularly interesting, however, is the appearance north and east of the masonry buildings of rows of workshops, neatly laid out but rather poorly built and with quantities of metalworking debris strewn on the rough clay floors. Is this evidence of more workshops, on an estate similar to Gestingthorpe, where agriculture was not the sole industry?

Other such estates may have existed. At Earl Stonham outside *Combretovium*, a villa lay on the south side of the river Gipping, while on the north bank an extensive scatter of occupation debris has been recorded. At Halstead a suspected villa is surrounded by a wide area strewn with domestic rubbish where at least two kilns are known. It is possible that this was a villa estate associated with pottery production. Further estate centres are suspected at Chadwell St. Mary and East Tilbury. Extensive areas of settlement are known from both these sites, although the evidence for villas is slight — at Chadwell St. Mary a plain red tessellated floor north-east of the site by the church, and at East Tilbury another tessellated floor near East Tilbury church.[25]

These villas just mentioned may have been modest structures occupied by a bailiff. Such may also have been the case at Wickford, where Mr. Rodwell has excavated part of a sprawling settlement which grew up at the road centre. Metalworking activities as well as agriculture left traces on the site, which was probably centred on a villa.

Many questions remain unanswered. In particular, how large were the areas farmed by the villas, and the estates? Only five field systems have so far been recognised from the canton, and these are only partially known. A system of enclosures is still being uncovered at Mucking on marginal

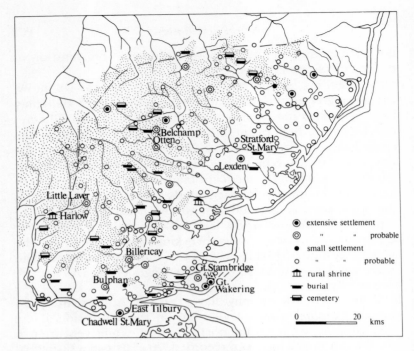

Fig. 29. Rural settlement, other than villas, in the canton

land overlooking the Thames. At Wendon's Ambo a small area of terraced rectangular fields was cut on the west slope of the Cam valley. At North Shoebury an extensive area of Iron Age and Roman enclosures and drove ways is currently being investigated, while part of a further field system is known at Little Waltham. The villas at Lidgate, Little Dunmow, and possibly Stebbing (Porter's Hall) apparently stood in ditched enclosures, and aerial photography has revealed a series of large enclosures at Gosbecks farm, south-west of Colchester.[26]

Peasant settlements

As can be seen from the distribution map (fig. 25) most of the villas stood on the lower slopes of valleys, where the clay was replaced by gravels. This siting was doubtless largely due to the presence of fresh water, but, as in the Belgic period, the lighter and better drained gravels were probably preferred for actual settlement.

A glance at fig. 29, however, shows equally clearly that in the Roman period rural settlement was by no means confined to the gravels — the dense forest that covered the clay lands must have been continuously eaten into as the Roman period advanced. Nor were the villas by any means the only form of rural settlement; on the contrary, the bulk of the Trinovantes must have lived in settlements far poorer and more ephemeral. Although these poorer communities established themselves on the river and glacial gravels, many are found on the clay soils also, presumably in clearings in the forest, while others are scattered along the coastal alluvial belt.

Recent fieldwork makes it clear that these poorer rural settlements sometimes consisted of quite large, sprawling clusters of timber huts covering several hectares. At Bulphan in central Essex a site covering about 15 acres (6 ha.) was excavated in the last century. About twenty 'shallow pits' 3-12 m. in diameter were found, filled with black soil. The larger examples may well have been accumulations of occupation material or household rubbish which had built up on the floors of circular huts, in which case we have here traces of a sizeable settlement occupied for 200 years. A similar settlement seems to have existed at Great Wakering, where pottery covers the entire Roman period, while what appears in the absence of excavation to be comparable occupation at Little Laver, Norsey Wood Billericay, and Belchamp Otton shows that these sites were not confined to south Essex; indeed they were widespread in Essex and Suffolk (fig. 29).

The comparatively low standard of living on some rural sites has been demonstrated by the excavations at Chadwell St. Mary. Here a complex of small ditches and rubbish pits containing late first and second century pottery was uncovered, and the excavator concluded that he was on the edge of an extensive settlement hardly touched by Romanising influences. A nearby cemetery produced generally rather poor grave-goods, although occasional luxuries occurred — an *amphora* and a samian dish among them. At East Tilbury four circular timber huts were excavated many years ago on the foreshore. Three of them were 6 m. in diameter; the fourth was smaller and may have been used as an

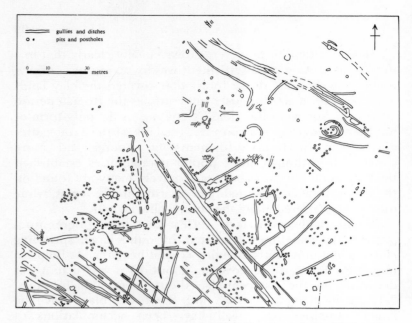

Fig. 30. Plan of the rural site at North Shoebury (after Macleod)

outbuilding. All were built of timber with daub coatings, but
the frequent occurrence of tiles suggests that at least some of
the roofs were tiled. The pottery from the site can be dated
to the later first and second centuries.

Recent excavations at North Shoebury, by Mr. Macleod,
have revealed an extensive area covered by a maze of pits,
post holes, ditches and gullies. Many of these date from the
early Iron Age, but associated pottery indicates that some of
the features are later and that the site was occupied
throughout Roman times and even into the sub-Roman
period (fig. 30).

The commonest type of rural settlement in the canton
may well have been the small farmstead. Many sites have
been recorded where modest amounts of pottery, tiles, food
bones and sometimes a few coins or other small finds have
been noted. Unfortunately none has yet been fully excavated.

Aerial photography has produced evidence for small
farmsteads near the Essex/Suffolk border. At Moat Farm,
Lexden, west of Colchester, a rectangular enclosure approxi-

Fig. 31. Enclosure at Moat Farm, Lexden. Moat Farm Dyke, a continuation of the Lexden Dyke, is marked by the line of the hedge to the top right

mately 90 m. wide but of unknown length was photographed by Professor St.Joseph (fig. 31). It lies on a south facing slope overlooking the Colne. A more extensive though similar site was discovered by local archaeologists at Stratford St. Mary in 1972. Here a rectangular enclosure, approximately 325 x 100 m., was divided into half. The northern half seems to be partly occupied by a large rectangular building, perhaps the farmhouse, although the plan is very simple. Two other large, less well-defined enclosures show on the photograph, one south-east of the main enclosure, the other impingeing on the western edge of the main enclosure. The relative dates of the enclosures are not known. Here again no excavation has been carried out, but the plan is very like that of the Romano-British farmsteads known elsewhere. Many more such settlements doubtless await discovery in our area.

Certainly the Trinovantian canton was densely occupied in the Roman period, and many of the scatters of Romano-British material noted by local archaeologists must mark similar homesteads, or in the case of larger collections, sprawling rural settlements. It is the excavation of these sites that would tell us of the everyday life of the average Trinovantian in Roman times; the lack of such excavation holds up our understanding not only of the lot of the ordinary people, but of the whole economic and social life of the Trinovantes.

The territorium of the colonia

Normally, and particularly under the republic and early empire, a *colonia* was surrounded by a *territorium* — a tract of agricultural land which was alloted to the settlers in the *colonia*, each colonist receiving an exact amount according to a fixed scale.

As a *colonia* Colchester probably had a *territorium* attached to it, although in the pre-Boudiccan period Trinovantian territory may have been classed as *agri captivi*. In this case colonists would have been able to seize at will as much native land as they wanted and to repeat the process as their need arose.[27] It is possible that one of the reforms initiated after the Boudiccan revolt was the provision of a fixed and permanent *territorium* for the *colonia*.

In the *territorium* of a *colonia* the Roman system of precise land division, or centuriation, would normally be applied. Under this system a tract of land was divided up into a regular 'chessboard' grid, consisting of squares or *centuriae* of identical size. The system was laid out from two roads or primary base lines, while the individual *centuriae* were bounded and subdivided by numerous secondary roads or tracks which both delimited the *centuriae* and provided them with access. Each colonist would be allotted a fixed number of *centuriae*, or of the smaller divisions within them. In parts of Italy and north Africa aerial photography has revealed extensive *territoria* where centuriation survives on a truly impressive scale.[28] Although attempts have been made to demonstrate a system of centuriation around Colchester none has yet gained general approval.

A striking feature of the immediate neighbourhood of Colchester is the two parallel roads west of the *colonia*. The main road, Stane Street, joined the London road at Marks

Tey, 8 km. outside the town. A second road however ran only 2,200 m. south of Stane Street. This branched off the London road at Easthorpe and headed east for 3.5 km. in the direction of Gosbecks, but its course beyond this has never been traced. It has been suggested that this curious arrangement may have resulted from a system of centuriation and that the two roads are all that remain of *limites* between *centuriae*. The distance of 2,200 m. between the two roads, however, does not really fit in with any likely scheme of centuriation.[29]

Similar attempts to show that surviving roads were part of a centuriation system have been made concerning the two main roads which run north-east/south-west across central Essex, that is the roads from Chigwell to Great Dunmow and Chelmsford to Braintree, short stretches of which, just south of Stane Street, run roughly parallel to each other. Apart from the roads themselves, however, there is no evidence for such a widespread system of centuriation as the argument implies, and again the spacing of these roads fits in with no known scheme of centuriation.[30]

The question of the extent of any *territorium* attached to the *colonia* is one that is particularly difficult to answer. Even in cases where remains of centuriation are well preserved, it has often been impossible to determine the size of the *territorium* attached to a particular town. Clearly the size of *territoria* differed greatly from place to place; the grants of land made to the original colonists were not invariably the same,[31] but it seems likely that the normal figure in the late republic and early empire was 50 *iugera* (about 31 acres or 12.6 ha.) to each settler. This is an arbitrary figure and in any case some settlers, for instance centurions, might receive more than others. If 4,000 colonists at Colchester were each allotted 50 *iugera*, however, about 500 square km. (an area slightly less than 200 square miles) would be needed. This would cover a radius of about 12 km. from the *colonia*, if the adjacent land were used. A slightly more generous distribution would include the 21 villas mentioned above (p. 99) which lie within 20 km. of the *colonia*. Their generally early foundations would suggest that they may have been occupied by colonists rather than

natives. However, as already suggested, the conquerors'
occupation of their lands may not have been confined to any
specific area, nor may it have been thought necessary to draw
up a formal plan of centuriation.

The rural shrines

Votive objects and the remains of small temples are by no
means uncommon from the canton. They have been recorded
from small towns and rural settlements from all parts of the
Trinovantian territory. Among these widespread shrines,
however, two are outstanding: the rural religious sites at
Gosbecks and Harlow.

The pre-Roman shrine at Gosbecks, 3.5 km. south-west of
Colchester, has been mentioned in chapter 1. It continued to
be venerated in the Roman period. In the late first century a
Romano-Celtic temple was erected within the Iron Age
enclosure and was surrounded by three masonry walls (fig.
32). It must be from this temple that the fine bronze
statuette of Mercury, now in the Colchester Museum,
originated. The statuette dates from the second century and,
standing 51 cm. high, is one of the finest bronzes known
from Roman Britain; it was ploughed up in 1945 at a point
roughly 30 m. north-east of the temple.[32]

Although doubtless the focus of the entire site, the temple
was only one of a number of large buildings. Two hundred
metres south of the temple was a theatre, originally built in
timber in the late first century and encased in a masonry shell
about fifty years later. The theatre was dismantled in the
early third century, but the rest of the site seems to have
been used until the fourth century.[33] Masonry remains have
been recorded in the field west of the temple where flue tiles
suggest the presence of a bath suite. Burials have been
recorded from the valley on the south-east margin of the site,
and traces of metal working have been found south of the
theatre (fig. 33).

Although extensive buildings doubtless existed here, no
streets have been recorded, apart from the Colchester to
Heybridge road which runs past the site on the west. Nor
have any domestic buildings ever been uncovered. There is

Fig. 32. Aerial photograph of the Gosbecks temple site

consequently no evidence that Gosbecks was a town, or even a permanent settlement, and it is better interpreted as a large rural fairground or market, of the type well known in Gaul. There, some two dozen sites have been recognised, where expensive public buildings — temples, baths, *mansiones*, and theatres — occur, but where the regular street grid, *forum, basilica*, private houses and defences of a town are lacking.[34] Altogether these sites seem to have been occupied only sporadically, but then by large numbers of people, and this has led to their interpretation as rural fairgrounds, which grew up around a shrine, attracting large numbers of pilgrims at times of festival.

Rural centres like Gosbecks may not have been uncommon in Roman Britain, but so far only a few have been recognised.[35] The Trinovantian canton, however, has produced another example, at Harlow. As at Gosbecks, the importance of Harlow as a religious centre started in pre-Roman times and continued throughout the Roman period. The Iron Age shrine drew pilgrims from a wide area, and was replaced by a modest winged Romano-Celtic temple

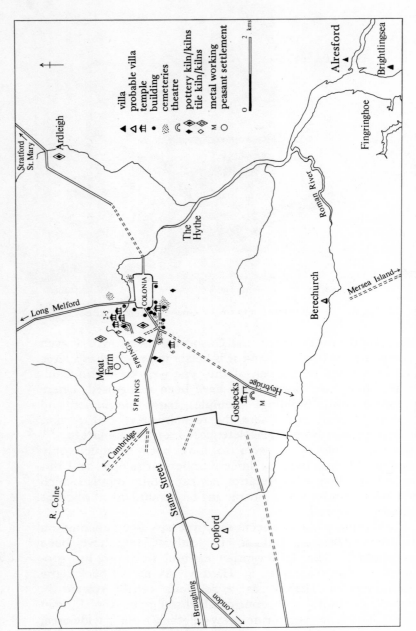

Fig. 33. Colchester and its environs

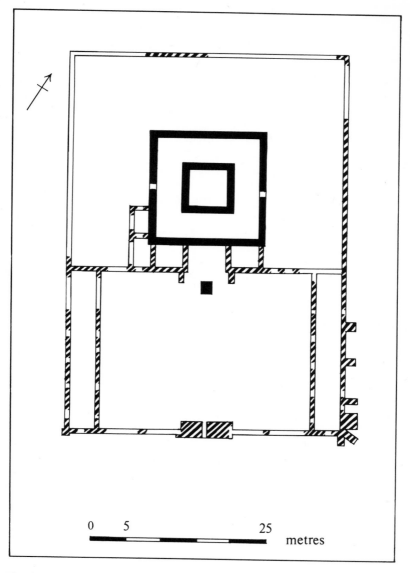

0   5   25
                                    metres

Fig. 34. Plan of the temple at Harlow in the third century with Flavian
walls in black, and third century walls hatched (after France
and Gobel)

in the later first century. Subsequently this temple was steadily embellished and enlarged. By the mid second century a large *temenos* covered one end of the prominent ridge on which the temple stood. On the lower slopes and at the base of the ridge, Roman remains, including traces of substantial buildings and small smithies, have been recorded, and it appears that by the later Roman period some permanent occupation had been established. At the northern end of the ridge, that is at the opposite end to that on which the temple stood, is a semi-circular depression which Mr. Hull suspected might have marked the position of a theatre *cavea*. Excavations on the site by the West Essex Archaeological Group, however, revealed no trace of any Roman structure here. Nevertheless, in spite of the relatively small amount of fieldwork and excavation that has yet been possible at Harlow and the consequent absence of positive information, it looks as if another rural market-place, comparable to that at Gosbecks, once stood here. It is worth remembering that the Gallic fairgrounds often lay on tribal frontiers and Harlow lies near what must have been the boundary between the Trinovantes and the Catuvellauni (fig. 34).[36]

Summary

Many of the villas in the canton must have developed only very gradually as local farmers accumulated wealth and steadily built up their farms, but some villas, particularly those around Colchester, were already comfortable and occasionally luxurious establishments before the end of the first century. The owners of these early villas may have been immigrant colonists based at Colchester, but the rich burials that occur at about the same time, over the belt of country which appears to have been the heart of the Trinovantian canton in the Belgic period, carry on an established native tradition and imply that some rich Trinovantian estates, presumably those of a pro-Roman party, survived both the Roman conquest and the Boudiccan revolt. In the Roman period the relationship between these aristocratic Trinovantes and the rest of the tribe is uncertain. Prior to the Roman conquest there would have been a strong social structure binding rich and poor together by mutual ties, involving obligations and kinship, which presumably continued to operate in the Roman period. In the absence of sufficient extensive excavation, the relationship between the aristocratic estates and the large rural settlements, which may loosely be termed villages, cannot yet be determined, but it may not be stretching the evidence too far to suggest that some 'villages' were populated by tenant farmers associated with a nearby villa. Gestingthorpe and Rivenhall are obvious potential examples. Late in the Roman period such tenant farmers might become *coloni*, serfs tied to large rural estates. Alongside the villages, however, were single homesteads and farms, presumably owned by independent peasant farmers, which might in time develop into villas.

As has been pointed out in a previous chapter, it is extremely difficult to distinguish between villages and small towns. The small towns usually had roots going back to the Belgic period, when they were obviously part of a purely rural economy, and throughout the Roman period they were closely linked with the agricultural life of the surrounding area. We may assume that the small towns acted primarily as market centres, although they might also be used as collecting posts for the *annona* and local administrative centres where, among other things, officials of the *cursus publicus* could be housed in a *mansio*. Villages on the other hand would be simply settlements of farmers concerned solely with agriculture.

Much more excavation and research is required before anything approaching an overall picture of the whole inter-related social and economic structure covering both town and country can be achieved. In the mean time it is often impossible to decide whether an individual site should be classed as a small town or as a rural settlement, while in the absence of even one totally excavated villa complex, small town, or peasant settlement from the canton, any overall reconstruction of the rural economy would be simply conjectural.

5.

Industry and the Economy

In a much-quoted passage, the geographer Strabo lists hides, cattle, corn, hunting dogs and slaves as among the principal British exports in the years prior to the Roman Conquest.[1] Since the time of Caesar, the Trinovantes had enjoyed close trading links with Rome, and all these could easily have come from the canton.

The glacial drift that covers much of Essex and south Suffolk gives rise to fertile loams, and grain growing has long been an important industry. The ear of barley on Cunobelin's coins attests the importance of the crop in the pre-Roman period, while grains of wheat have been recorded on several Roman sites.[2] The twelve enormous iron scythes, possibly part of a reaping machine or *vallus*, which were found in a hoard of ironwork at Great Chesterford,[3] point to grain production on a large scale, as do the millstone pivot and other remains of a water mill found in the same hoard (fig. 35). Corn-drying ovens have been found at Ridgewell, Heydon, Hadstock, Rivenhall, Billericay, Wickford and Mucking, while a large pit probably intended for grain storage has been excavated at Wickford[4] and what has been interpreted as a grain grinding area at Gestingthorpe.[5] Querns are common all over the canton.

In addition to arable farming, stock raising must have formed an important part of the Trinovantian economy, while the extensive woodlands provided valuable pannage for swine. Both cattle and swine had considerable economic importance in Roman times. Pork and bacon played an important part in the military diet, and doubtless also in the

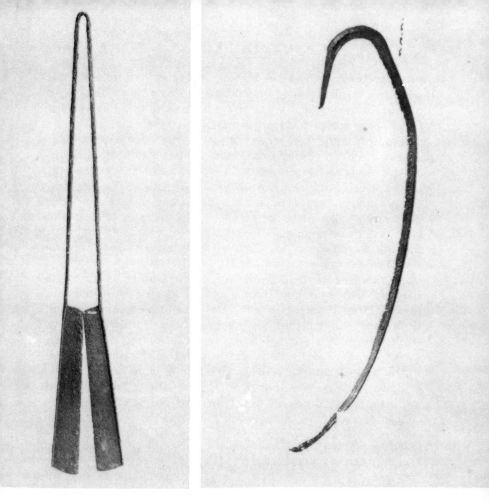

Fig. 35. Iron blade and cropping shears from the hoard of ironwork at Great Chesterford

civilian one. Beef was also popular among both civilians and the army, while leather was extensively used for clothing, and above all by the army for tents and uniforms. There is some evidence for stock raising on imperial estates,[6] which may have partially met army requirements, but even so civilian needs would have been considerable.

As we saw in the last chapter, in the part of the canton pre-eminently suited to stock raising, that is the clay lands of south and central Essex, villas are scarce. It must be remembered however that there is a scattering of villas along the gravels of the Thames Valley, and as any estate concerned with stock raising would need large tracts of land, the owners of the Thames-side villas may have had ranches reaching north, over south and central Essex.

The probable existence of sheep-runs in parts of East Anglia has been commented on in the past,[7] and the presence in the Great Chesterford iron-work hoard of large shears, used for cropping the nap on woollen cloth in the final stage of its manufacture, is positive evidence for cloth manufacture on a large scale in the area (fig. 35). In the later Middle Ages, Colchester and many of the villages of north Essex and south Suffolk were famous for their woollen industry, and this may also have been the case in the Roman period.

At the time of the compilation of the Domesday Book, the Essex marshes in the Dengie and Tendring Hundreds supported large flocks of sheep, and in the Mediaeval period a flourishing cheese industry using sheeps' milk grew up,[8] while the area around Tilbury was supporting thousands of sheep in the eighteenth century when Defoe journeyed through the county.[9] Although there is little archaeological evidence, it is not impossible that sheep were already important in southern Essex in the Roman period. The cheese presses from Sheepen and Heybridge could as well be evidence of sheep rearing as of dairy farming. At Mucking small sub-rectilinear enclosures of Belgic date have been interpreted by the excavator as sheep folds.[10]

A natural product which has not received much attention is timber. In Roman times much of the canton was densely wooded (above, p. 3). London in particular, and to a lesser extent Colchester, would have required large quantities of constructional timber. Furthermore, this timber would need to be carefully cut and seasoned; we may judge from the carpenters' tools that survive how high was the standard of Romano-British carpentry. All this would demand skill and business acumen. A London builder would not simply go to the forest and cut wood; he is more likely to have dealt through timber merchants who accrued profits of their own. Indeed the hinterland of London, part of which lay in south Essex, must have been stimulated in many ways by the day-to-day needs of the provincial capital.

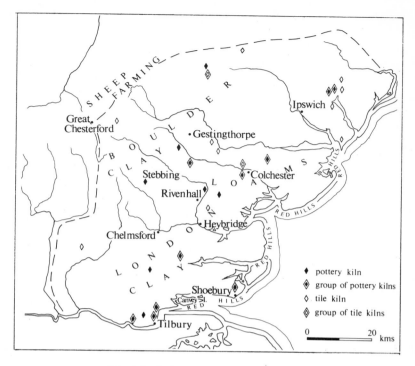

Fig. 36. Industrial sites in the canton

Fishing and sea-borne trade

Many of the villas, particularly in the Colchester area, lie on the coast. Alresford, Fingringhoe, Brightlingsea, St. Osyth and Mersea are very close to navigable water, while in the south of the canton there is evidence for a string of villas on the gravel terraces overlooking the Thames estuary. In Suffolk the villa on Castle Hill, Ipswich, overlooks the Stour and Gipping estuaries. It is difficult to escape the conclusion that the sea played an important part in the lives of these villa owners. Along the Essex coast, the oyster industry probably held an important place in the local economy, as indeed it continued to do until the present century. Villages such as Mersea and Brightlingsea relied heavily on coastal fishing and the oyster industry. The widespread occurrence of oyster shells on Romano-British sites is evidence in itself for the popularity of this delicacy, but there is also

documentary evidence. Tacitus mentions British pearls, albeit
rather scathingly, and they appear again in late Roman
literature, while Pliny and Juvenal both refer to British
oysters.[11] Colchester is still famous for locally produced
oysters, and oyster shells are prolific on sites from the Belgic
period onwards. As one would expect, they belong to the
Colchester 'native' variety, a type unique to the Colne
estuary. Other shell-fish were also eaten. On the Sheepen site
small quantities of mussel and cockle shells were found
among the vast quantities of oyster shells in the mid first
century middens. The shells of these smaller varieties were so
powdered as to be not immediately discernible, but they may
originally have formed an appreciable percentage of the total
quantity of shell-fish eaten. The shell-fish industry was
doubtless both well organised and profitable.[12]

Fish bones have been noted on excavations in Colchester,
and these, together with imported *amphorae*, some of which
contained highly-flavoured fish sauces, remind us of the
importance of fish in the Roman diet. It is not surprising that
we find villas so closely connected with sea water and on
creeks which could provide havens for fishing craft.

There can be little doubt that the coastal position of the
Trinovantes provided incentives for trade, both coastal and
with the Continent. Ipswich, Colchester and Maldon are still
ports today, and were thriving and prosperous in the Middle
Ages. Only at Heybridge have traces of wharves been
found,[13] but it is more than likely that these await discovery
at Colchester. Trade links between Colchester and the
Continent received an early boost when quantities of glass,
samian and fine pottery were brought into the early *colonia*,
and these imports were doubtless maintained after the revolt.
The large quantities of exotic building materials used to
embellish the court of the Temple of Claudius were surely
brought by sea direct to Colchester. Later on the Colchester
pottery industry expanded, but it was the town's position as
a port that was responsible for the location here of the
short-lived samian pottery kilns in the late second century,
which relied on clay imported in bulk from the Continent. At
about the same time, *mortaria* were supplied to the units on
the northern frontier from the Colchester kilns; it is easier to

envisage this pottery transported north by sea than by pack-horse.

Ports doubtless existed in the south of the canton, but as yet they have not been precisely located, although Tilbury, Canvey Island, Southend, Shoebury, Great Wakering and Burnham-on-Crouch have all produced collections of Roman material which may well mark the sites of harbours.[14]

Salt manufacture

An important product of the sea-shore was salt. All along the Essex coast from the Thames to Walton, but particularly in south Essex, are low irregularly shaped mounds known locally as 'red hills'. Well over 150 of these are already known and many more must await discovery. They are usually 0.75-1.50 m. high and generally occur in small groups covering areas of between half an acre and thirty acres (0.2-12 ha.). For many years the construction and use of these mounds was uncertain, but they are now thought to be the accumulated debris produced during salt working. Recent excavations have been undertaken by the Colchester Archaeological Group on red hills at Maldon and Peldon and the following account is based largely on their finds (fig. 37).[15]

The Maldon red hill covered 3.9 acres (1.6 ha.) on a site which in Roman times would have been a low clay island, lying in mud flats and liable to be covered by the sea during storms and spring tides. Some sort of firm surface must nevertheless have existed, on which the salt producing processes took place, so it is not surprising that some half dozen working floors, roughly made surfaces incorporating clay lumps, were uncovered in the excavation.

Red hills excavated in the past have proved to be made up of accumulations of burnt earth, including a small proportion of *briquetage*, or broken pieces of fired clay, sometimes in shapeless lumps and sometimes made up of parts of bars. pedestals and containers of various shapes. No complete vessel has yet been restored. The Maldon red hill was no exception to this general rule. Domestic refuse is not uncommon in red hills and is often of Iron Age, Belgic or early Roman date although later Roman material has sometimes been recorded.

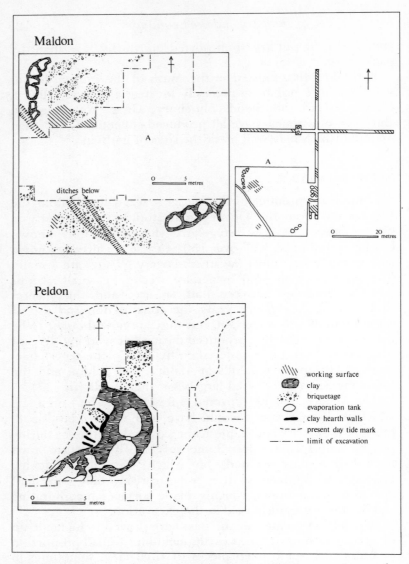

Maldon

A

0   5
metres

ditches below

Peldon

A

O   20
metres

working surface
clay
briquetage
evaporation tank
clay hearth walls
present day tide mark
limit of excavation

O   5
metres

Fig. 37. Excavated features in the red hills at Maldon and Peldon (after
de Brisay)

Red hills are often situated at roughly the high tide-mark
in Roman times, and at Maldon pits 1.25 m. in diameter and
15 cm. deep, lined with raw clay, were dug at about the tidal
limit (fig. 38). Sea water was apparently let into these pits

Fig. 38. Evaporation tanks in the Osea Road, Maldon, red hill

and left to evaporate until a deposit of brine was left. This brine must have been finally dried off in the large containers already mentioned.

Resting on many working surfaces in the Maldon red hill were the remains of rough pedestals, whose bases were wedged into the working surfaces, while the heads supported fire bars on which were placed the drying containers. Fires were lit on the working surfaces beneath the containers to complete the crystallisation of the brine. Intense heat must have been generated, as some of the Maldon floors were burnt to a depth of 6 cm., and in places the clay had become vitrified. Vitrified clay has been recorded from several red hills. It is clear, however, that the process varied; at Peldon no pedestals were found, but instead, hearth walls with traces of fire bars on them.

Although the excavation of the Maldon red hill has shed much light on the problem of red hills, many questions remain unanswered. For how long were individual red hills used? How much salt would have been produced on one site? Clearly some of the larger red hills represent sites that were used for some time or where a large quantity of salt was produced. One puzzling aspect of red hills is the decline in their numbers in the later Roman period. Salt was a valuable commodity and its production an important factor in the tribal economy. It may be that the decline in red hill formation results from the introduction of novel salt panning techniques. Is it possible that in the third century the state began to exercise more control over the salt working, bringing in new techniques which did not result in the formation of pronounced red hills?

Pottery manufacture

Both the pottery and the tile industry played an important part in the tribal economy. Pre-eminent in this sphere was Colchester, where over thirty pottery kilns are already known and where more doubtless await discovery. They almost surround the town, but are most numerous on its western side, in the Hilly and Warren Fields. We saw in chapter 2 how the pre-Roman site at Sheepen was converted into an industrial area serving the Claudian fort and early *colonia*, providing an early impetus which may well have been responsible for the location of the later industry here. The Hilly and Warren Fields have many natural advantages, however, notably the combination of deposits of clay, suitable for both tiles and pottery, in the Colne valley, and a well drained gravel and sand site further up the slope. Wood for firing the kilns must also have been plentiful. These factors may well have led to the siting of Belgic kilns here. Much of the vast quantity of pottery found on the Sheepen site and dating to the decades prior to the Roman conquest must have been made locally, and although no kilns have yet been found, their discovery is doubtless merely a matter of time (see fig. 33).[16]

After the Roman conquest kilns were promptly established on the Sheepen site. Kiln 26, specialising in the production of flagons, jugs and bowls,[17] was apparently destroyed in A.D. 60. The eighty flagons found in the storehouse in *insula* 10 of the *colonia* (above, p. 50) are of the same type as those in Kiln 26, while the *mortaria* in the store may also have been

Fig. 39. The Colchester Vase, doubtless a product of the local kilns

made locally.[18] It must be borne in mind, however, that these early Roman potters were not necessarily Trinovantes. Quintus Veranius Secundus (or Severus), whose name appears stamped on many of the *mortaria* from the storehouse, was presumably a Roman citizen, and may have been a foreign business man who came here in the wake of the Roman army, and the very presence of novel Romano-British pottery kilns implies the influence of foreign craftsmen. The pottery

found in the Boudiccan destruction layer in the *colonia*,
however, is on the whole very similar to that in use on the
native site at Sheepen, although there are minor differences
in the popularity of certain types on the two sites.

After the Boudiccan revolt, the kilns were probably
re-established, although so far late-first century kilns are
lacking. From the mid second century onwards the pottery
industry flourished and in the later decades of the century at
least one samian kiln was established; a venture which proved
unsatisfactory, probably due to the high price of the ware
coupled with the difficulties encountered by its makers in
firing it properly. Other branches of the industry flourished,
however, particularly those concerned with the production of
mortaria and fine colour coated wares (fig. 39), and kilns
continued to be established outside Colchester right down
until the end of the fourth century.[19]

Unlike much of the industry of Roman Britain, which was
based on small workshops run by individual craftsmen, the
Colchester kilns were on occasion organised on a larger scale.
Seven kilns, excavated in 1933,[20] were apparently all the
property of one firm which operated in the late second
century. Four kilns, including the highly specialised samian
kiln, lay within a walled enclosure; the remains of three more
lay nearby but outside the wall. Other structures found
nearby included a clay dump, an oven and a platform
possibly used to facilitate the loading of wagons. The seven
kilns had been used to fire an enormous variety of wares.
Apart from the samian kiln, where both plain and decorated
samian ware was produced (fig. 40), colour coated beakers,
mortaria, lamps, flagons, dishes, bowls and cooking pots were
manufactured, together with occasional exotic pieces. Much
of the samian and *mortaria* and a small proportion of the
colour coated beakers were stamped with the potter's name,
and from these a list of twenty-six potters has been compiled,
fourteen of whom were making samian ware. Clearly a
sizeable firm operated here.

The Colchester market was naturally supplied with the
products of the local kilns. Comparatively little of this
pottery however is found on other sites in Essex and Suffolk,
where its place is taken by more locally made coarse wares,

Fig. 40. Mould for a samian bowl from the Colchester samian kiln

often similar in form to types found at Colchester, but made in different fabric. The fine wares, particularly in the late Roman period, may come from districts other than Colchester, and the products of the Oxford and Nene Valley kilns are well represented.[21] In settlements as near to Colchester as Chelmsford and even Kelvedon, the pottery differs from that at Colchester, and it is clear that these places were at any rate in part supplied by their own kilns. In the second century, and perhaps at other periods too, Colchester supplied a distant market on the northern frontier with *mortaria*, while the products of the samian kilns spread beyond tribal frontiers.

Turning away from Colchester, a large kiln site has recently been investigated at Hasketon. Occupation on the site began in the Belgic period but it was not until after the conquest that pottery production began on quite a large scale. Traces of a large number of kilns have been recognised but at the time of writing little excavation has been possible. There are indications that many kilns still await discovery here. The pottery produced was coarse grey cooking pots and storage jars, but the scale of manufacture suggests that they must have spread over a wide area. Tile kilns were also represented. The site thrived for about a century before being abandoned in the early Antonine period.

On the whole however, potteries were small-scale and usually consisted of only a few kilns, probably supplying at most only a limited area and generally simply one settlement. Such kilns would produce the coarse wares for the settlement, fine ware being imported from Colchester or elsewhere.

At Ardleigh, 6.5 km. north-east of Colchester, two kilns dating from the late first to early second century produced coarse grey cooking pots and carinated bowls. This must have been the cheapest type of domestic pottery, and it is interesting to note that although the carinated bowls are frequently found in the contemporary rubbish pits, they occur only rarely in graves. They were obviously considered unsuitable as burial gifts.

In south Essex small groups of kilns have been excavated at Rettenden (where late fourth century pottery, including flanged bowls, was made and distributed over a wide area from Chelmsford to the Thames), at West Tilbury, Grays and Shoebury. These produced pottery for local use, as must also be the case with the rural kilns at Halstead, Mucking, Sible Hedingham, Sicklesmere, Chadwell St. Mary and Martlesham, to name but a few.[22] A possible kiln site lies at Belchamp Otton where in one part of an extensive site pits 'like crude kilns' were recorded in 1950. In view of the recent excavations at Rushden of early Roman kilns consisting simply of small pits and fire bars, it is possible that the pits at Belchamp Otton were the remains of similar kilns.[23]

The extensive clay lands in the canton gave rise to a large number of tile kilns. Many of these must have had a very limited life and simply supplied the needs of one building or settlement. Such must have been the function of isolated tile kilns at Braxted, Alphamstone, Ashdon, Bures, Elmswell, Trimley St. Mary and Theydon Garnon.[24] Rather larger groups of tile kilns, however, occur at Wissington, Melton and Pettistree,[25] while the very extensive remains at Stanningfield suggest the existence of a brick or tile factory; no settlement is known in the immediate vicinity, so presumably the kilns' products were traded over some distance. The occurrence in the canton of decorated flue tiles made in Surrey reminds us how extensive was the tile trade. Even rich clay lands like the Trinovantian canton imported specialised tiles.[26]

Minor industries

Doubtless every small settlement had its own blacksmith, if not its own bronze smith. Small scale iron and bronze smithies are known or inferred at Chadwell St. Mary, Colchester, Chelmsford, Kelvedon, *Combretovium* and Heybridge.[27] The blacksmith's workshop excavated at Chelmsford was a small smithy designed merely to meet the everyday demands of the local community and the same is true of the two small bronze smithies excavated at Colchester. In connection with the *colonia*, Professor Richmond long ago remarked on the absence of workshops compared with the situation in other major Romano-British towns.[28] This absence, however, may be more apparent than real — the result of limited excavation which further work may rectify.

An interesting feature of the canton is the existence of industry other than agriculture on a few villa sites. The workshops at Stebbing (above, p. 107) suggest that here metal-working was organised on a large scale, surely greater than that required by the needs of the villa alone, while at Gestingthorpe metal-working held an important position as the discovery of clay mould fragments for casting bronze statuettes testifies. Although these are the only examples known so far, they suggest that some of the richer villas in the canton were not solely based on agriculture. The existence of such establishments, employing skilled metal-workers, must have had a considerable effect on the local economy if this system was at all widespread.

Dozens of minor industries must have existed in the canton which have left little or no trace. Early in the Roman period bronze brooches of 'Colchester type' enjoyed a widespread distribution and many must have been made at Colchester. Glass was produced there, and the industry may date back to the late first century, if the letter C moulded on a glass bowl in one of the Bartlow *tumuli* does indeed refer to Colchester. Traces of lamp manufacture have been found in Colchester.[29] Leather-working must have been widespread although positive traces survive only rarely,[30] and the manufacture of bone objects was probably closely connected with this work.

It is clear from this survey that the Trinovantian economy was a rural one. Large-scale industry like the Colchester potteries was very much the exception; agriculture, supplemented by the produce of the sea and serviced by small workshops and smithies, formed the basis of the economy.

6.

The Late Fourth and Fifth Centuries

The Trinovantes, exposed as they were to sea-borne raiding, must have felt their full share of the events of 367, but, as with the rest of lowland Britain, there is little archaeological evidence of the disaster. Late Roman burning has been recorded at Wickford and Ixworth, but this could well have resulted from accidental fires and there is certainly no proof that it was the work of raiders in 367.[1] There is no sign of destruction either at the fort at Bradwell or on coastal villa sites such as Alresford, Ipswich and Tollesbury, in spite of their vulnerable positions, nor can we point to an increase in the number of hoards of coins or valuables buried at this date. Some two dozen late Roman coin hoards have been recorded from the canton, but there is no sudden increase in their numbers, such as might be explained by the danger and loss of life in 367-8.

As we saw in chapter 4, there is evidence pointing to the presence of a few large rural estates of the type that would have been worked by *coloni*, and it has been pointed out that the desertion of an estate by its workers could have led to as much chaos as the destruction of the villa itself,[2] although it would leave little trace in the archaeological record.

By 370 order had been established. This is not the place to describe the arrangements made by Count Theodosius to retrieve the northern frontier, but it is clear that he also took steps to improve the defences of the province further south, precautions that must have affected the Trinovantes with their long, exposed coastline. For several years distinctive late Roman military equipment, decorated with chip-carved patterns and employing designs ultimately based on zoomorphic motifs, has been recognised on numerous sites in lowland Britain.[3] This equipment consists of bronze buckles and belt fittings closely similar to examples found in late fourth century graves on the frontier of Gaul. The Gallic graves appear to be those of Germanic warriors and it is probable that the chip-carved metalwork of southern Britain reflects the presence here of Germanic mercenaries brought over after 367 by Theodosius to augment the provinces' ravished defences. The appearance of their bronze equipment as well as the occasional warrior grave, both in towns and on villa sites, demonstrates that now not only were the forts of the Saxon shore re-established, but for the first time towns, and even villas, were allotted detachments of troops.

The Trinovantian canton has produced several examples of this chip-carved metalwork. The loop of a buckle was found at Bradwell and although erosion has removed all the evidence at Walton Castle there is no reason to suppose that it was not also maintained after 367. Steps were taken to improve the defences of Colchester. A magnificent British-made chip-carved buckle (fig. 41) was found many years ago 'somewhere in the town' and more recently a bronze strap end of similar style was found on the surface of the London road 0.65 km. west of the town.[4] In addition there is a hint that Germanic mercenary graves may have been destroyed in the last century. A Victorian postman and amateur archaeologist, William Wire, kept a remarkably detailed diary between 1842 and his death in 1857, in which he recorded archaeological discoveries made in the town. Since this was the period during which the railway was laid, the town sewage system installed, extensive new suburbs built and new sandpits opened, his diaries provide a mine of information. In 1839 a new sandpit was started in Butt Road, about 200 m. south-west of the town. The work proceeded slowly in those unmechanised days, but Wire continually recorded the discovery of skeletons, generally accompanied by late Roman pottery and coins, but sometimes also by ironwork, particularly spears.[5] This sounds highly reminiscent of the cemetery outside Dorchester-on-Thames, for instance, where Germanic mercenaries were buried, accompanied by iron

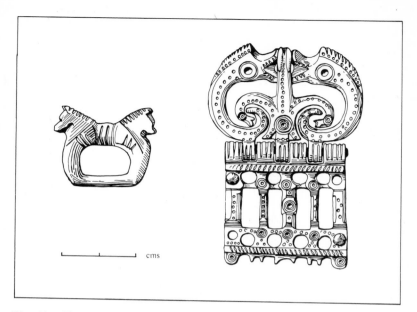

Fig. 41. Chip-carved metalwork from the canton, left: Gestingthorpe, right: Colchester (after Hawkes and Dunning)

weapons and chip-carved bronzes, and it seems likely that Colchester was also provided with a detachment of Germanic troops. It was once thought that the seven semi-circular bastions which project from the town wall on its south-east sector might also have been added in the late fourth century, but excavations on bastion 3 in 1965 proved once and for all that the Colchester bastions are mediaeval, probably dating from the late fourteenth century.

Colchester was not the only town in the area to be strengthened. At some time in the mid or late fourth century, Great Chesterford, on the western margin of the canton, was provided with an impressive town wall and ditch enclosing an area of about 35 acres (14 ha.). This substantial defence is clearly too expensive to have been paid for simply by the town's inhabitants unaided, and they must have been subsidised, at the very least, by the central government. The reason why such a comparatively small and poor settlement as Great Chesterford should have been defended at all is difficult to understand at first sight, but it may be that the town, lying as it does in the heart of rich agricultural land, was a regional depot or collecting point for the *annona*. The government would be anxious that this corn, essential for the army, should be well protected, while the period immediately after 367 seems the most likely one in which such steps would have been taken. It is interesting to note in this context that Major Brinson excavated a building of mid to late fourth century date which he thought might have been a small tax office.[7] In the south of the canton lies the only other town for which there is evidence for town walls, and although we have no proof since all trace of the walls has disappeared, it is probable that *Durolitum*, 'the walled town by the ford', was defended at the same time and for much the same reasons as Great Chesterford.

The Germanic mercenaries were not quartered solely in towns and forts. Items of the chip-carved equipment have been found on rural sites; at Mucking in the south of the canton, at Gestingthorpe, 22 km. north-west of Colchester (fig. 41), and at Ixworth and Icklingham on the border between the Iceni and Trinovantes. This suggests that some villas may have been allotted detachments of soldiers, perhaps sent to protect vital corn-producing estates. Most of the equipment from these rural find spots, however, was produced in Britain itself, probably at the very end of the fourth century or even later; the buckle from Gestingthorpe may have been made on the site, where there is earlier evidence that metal working had supplemented the agricultural economy.

The late Roman government employed barbarian mercenaries in a number of ways. They might serve in the army as regular but low grade troops, or whole tribal groups might be settled in frontier districts as *laeti* or *foederati*. It is not yet clear how many regular troops were brought into the canton, but certainly a number of *laeti* or *foederati* existed here before the main phase of Anglo-Saxon settlement in the mid fifth century.[8] A *laeti* settlement is being excavated at Mucking on a gravel terrace overlooking the Thames estuary 7 km. north-east of Tilbury. Occupation on the site lasted over hundreds of years, but one of its most interesting features was the early Anglo-Saxon settlement, comprising two cemeteries and over a hundred *grubenhauser* strung out for a kilometre along the terrace. Several of the *grubenhauser*

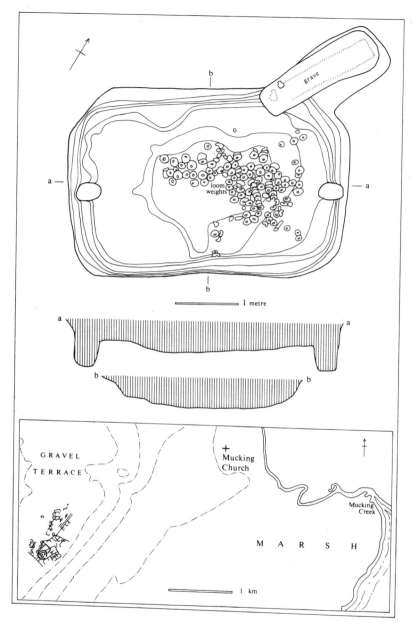

Fig. 42. A *grubenhaus* from Mucking (after Mrs. Jones)

have produced Anglo-Saxon pottery for which continental evidence suggests dates from the early fifth or possibly even the late fourth centuries. As we have already noted, late fourth and early fifth century chip-carved metalwork has also been found at Mucking, both in huts and graves, but it is clear from the presence of Germanic pottery, and indeed from the whole style of life on the site, that these early Anglo-Saxon settlers were not simply mercenaries but an entire community, presumably settled here as *laeti* to defend the approach to London (fig. 42).[9]

In addition to Mucking other settlements of *laeti* doubtless existed in the canton. To the north, on the edge of Icenian territory at West Stow, another early Anglo-Saxon village has recently been excavated which seems to have started life soon after 400.[10] Early Germanic pottery has also been recorded from Heybridge, where Mr. Drury has also uncovered early Anglo Saxon *grubenhauser*, Feering, Little Oakley, Rivenhall, Great Stambridge, Shoebury, Great Wakering, Rawreth, Wickford, Canvey Island and Gun Hill, Tilbury, where two further *grubenhauser* have been located.[11] At Inworth an Anglo-Saxon button brooch of early fifth century date has been found by Mr. Rodwell on a kiln site.[12] Early fifth century Germanic remains have been found immediately north-west of the canton in the Cambridge region. Since the pottery suggests the presence of women, traditionally the makers of pottery, these finds probably reflect the widespread distribution of *laeti* in the early fifth century.

How much does this situation reflect the settlement of 369? We have already seen that Theodosius may have been responsible for the defence of Great Chesterford and the presence of Germanic soldiery, but it is doubtful that *laeti* were introduced as early as this. Politically, however, the late fourth and early fifth centuries were an unsettled period for Britain and *laeti* could have been brought in at any time, although the aftermath of the events of 383 and the years around Stilicho's visit in 398 spring to mind as likely periods. On the other hand some *laeti* settlements probably date from the decades after 407-10, when the *civitates* of Britain seem to have continued the late Roman policy of settling barbarians in exposed districts.

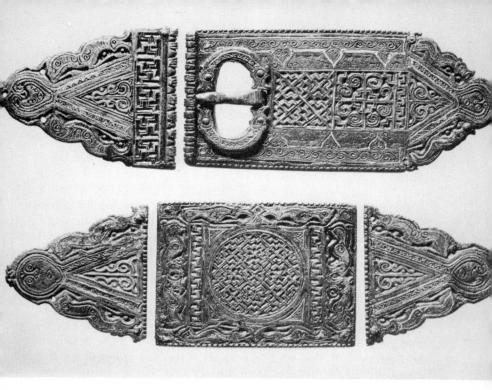

Fig. 43. Belt mounts of bronze inlaid with silver from grave 117, Saxon cemetery 1, Mucking

Whatever the initial date of the *laeti* settlements, it is clear that they were not uncommon in Trinovantian territory in the first half of the fifth century, and they must have made a considerable impact on the local population. It is true that all the available evidence suggests that the early Germanic settlers absorbed little or nothing of the culture of Roman Britain, but nevertheless the presence of the *laeti* must have been felt by the Trinovantes. What, for instance, were the relations between the newcomers and the villa owners? Were the Germanic settlers simply taking over deserted villa estates, or were they deliberately settled by the Trinovantes or by the provincial government on certain villa lands? Certainly there was a carefully planned defence system protecting the Thames estuary, of which Mucking was a part,[13] and elsewhere in the canton *laeti* may have been settled to defend the countryside as well as the towns. In certain parts of the canton, particularly in the south-east, large areas of land must have passed out of Trinovantian hands in the early fifth century.

As the fifth century proceeded new immigrants continually augmented the numbers of early Germanic settlers. Pottery at Snape, Rivenhall, Bulmer and Mucking has been dated by Dr. Myres to *c*. 440, and he has pointed out that it has Frisian and Jutish characteristics,[14] while at Mucking a five-piece set of belt fittings decorated in the Anglo-Saxon Quoit Brooch style but modelled on late fourth century chip-carved metalwork has been found (fig. 43). It has been suggested that fittings decorated in this style were made in Britain in the early fifth century for a wealthy, perhaps military, class with a taste for Germanic ornaments, who were invited into the country soon after 410.[15]

Of the Trinovantes themselves there is little trace and it is very difficult to distinguish early fifth century British occupation. After 370 fewer new coins reached the province and after 410 the supply ceased. With the collapse of the economy generally the great pottery industries came to an end. 'Sub-Roman' pottery has been recorded at Chelmsford and Great Dunmow,[16] but the dearth of early fifth century material makes it very difficult to recognise sites occupied at this period, although presumably the bulk of the local population continued living in their established homes.

In areas of central and southern Essex there are a number of place names incorporating the element *ingas* combined with an early Anglo-Saxon personal name and meaning the followers of a particular man, as for instance in Roding, the settlement of the men or followers of *Hroda*. Although in the past this type of place name has been thought to belong to the earliest phase of Anglo-Saxon settlement, it has been suggested recently that although it doubtless dates from an early phase, it represents a secondary colonisation taking place soon after the initial immigration. Thus in Essex early fifth century immigrants settled, or were settled, on the exposed coastal areas, particularly around the Thames estuary, and the earliest Germanic remains are commonest south and east of the London to Colchester road. The *ingas* place names, on the other hand, lie predominantly north and west of this line (fig. 44). In the light of this it may be

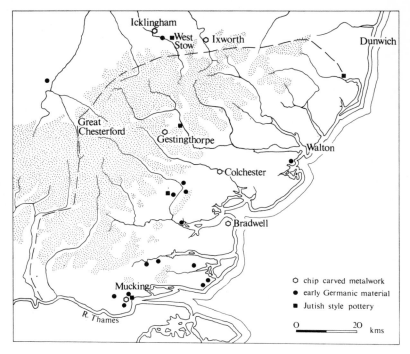

Fig. 44. Early fifth-century occupation in the canton

that in the latter area the Trinovantes carried on a late-Roman way of life in the early fifth century, while in south-east Essex Germanic settlements were proliferating. It was only later on, perhaps after 449, Bede's date for the arrival of the Saxons in the country, that the area of Germanic settlement spread over the whole canton.[17]

There is growing evidence for gradual and peaceful Saxon infiltration, and the slow collapse of the Romano-British way of life. There is hardly any evidence of violence or destruction. At Ixworth the villa was burnt down and never re-built,[18] although the precise date at which this happened remains uncertain and in any case the fire could well have been accidental. Less easily explained in these terms is the final fate of Duncan's Gate at Colchester.[19] Unfortunately much evidence on the later history of the gateway was destroyed in the last century by unscientific excavation, but it appears that this small postern gate ended its life in flames. This looks very like the result of a hostile and successful

attack, but so far there is no supporting evidence from the
town itself, where late-Roman houses seem to have crumbled
away through neglect and decay rather than meeting a more
dramatic end. It is possible that this was also the time when
the Balkerne Gate was blocked by a roughly built wall which
closed the north footway, both carriage ways, and probably
the south footway also.[20] The excavator thought that when
the blocking was put in, the gateway was already in ruins,
presumably as a result of neglect since no burnt layers have
been recorded, and a later Saxon date is generally preferred.
Within the town walls at Colchester a *grubenhaus* has
recently been excavated and has been dated to the fifth
century,[21] but we do not know how the earlier Roman
building on the site met its end, nor the relationship between
the Saxon inhabitants and the remnants of the Romano-
British population.

The evidence is admittedly slight but it suggests that in the
canton as a whole there was further barbarian settlement in
the first half of the fifth century. It is becoming clear that
after the termination of Roman government in 410, groups
of Saxons continued to come into the canton, probably at
the request of the Trinovantian leaders who were simply
continuing the established tradition of entrusting the defence
to *foederati* and *laeti*. Later on these barbarians came of their
own accord in the face of the now powerless Trinovantes,
until, by the middle of the century their numbers were too
great for the remaining Romano-British population to control.

Certainly by the sixth century the area which had once
formed the Trinovantian canton was a Saxon area rather than
a British enclave.[22] The way of life that emerges is a pagan
Saxon one, alien to the old established Romano-British
culture and as such outside the scope of this book. We do not
know what was the final fate of the Trinovantes; were they
absorbed by the Saxon population, or were they driven out
or exterminated? Suffice it to say that although there is little
sign of violence or destruction in the late fourth or early fifth
centuries, nevertheless the Trinovantes disappeared so completely that here the Celtic language has left fewer traces than
anywhere else in Britain.[23]

Notes and references

References to British journals use the abbreviations recommended by the Council for British Archaeology, which are those of the American Standards Association (list Z39,5-1963, revised 1966). Other abbreviations used are:

CMR   *Colchester Museum Report*
RIB   R.G. Collingwood and R.P. Wright *Roman Inscriptions of Britain* i (Oxford 1965)
VCH   *Victoria County History*

1. TRIBAL TERRITORY AND THE PRE-ROMAN IRON AGE

1. *VCH Essex*, i, 1-18 for a summary of drift geology based on nineteenth-century surveys. See also Wooldridge and Linton *1933* for a discussion of early settlement on brickearths.
2. Wheeler *1929* and Cunliffe *1968b*, 224.
3. *VCH Essex* i, 337-80.
4. At Mucking a large group of round huts, in two cases set in compounds, has been excavated by Mrs. Jones. For occupation at Linford Quarry, Mucking, Barton *1962*; at Wickford, Rodwell *1971* and *1972c*. Part of a single circular hut was excavated by the writer at Witham in 1970, and further examples are known at Butley (Ipswich Museum) and Ardleigh (Erith and Holbert *1970*). Early Iron Age occupation was recorded in the last century at Walthamstow, *Archaeol. J.* xxxv (1876), 170. Above all see Clarke *1940* and *1960*, and Drury *1973*. A full report on Little Waltham is forthcoming.
5. Cunliffe *1968a*.
6. *VCH Essex* i, 277 (Loughton), 278-9 (Ambresbury Banks), 280 (Wallbury and Littlebury), 284 (Asheldham). *Proc. Cambridge Antiq. Soc.* l (1957), 7-27 (Wandlebury) and lvii (1963), 9-29 (Cherry Hinton). For Saffron Walden, *Trans. Essex Archaeol. Soc.*

i, 2 (3rd series), 141-50. See also the Ordnance Survey *Map of Southern Britain in the Iron Age.*

7. Information from Mr. Macleod on Great Stambridge, Mrs. Jones on Mucking, and Mr. Drury on Heybridge. Major collections of early Iron Age material are also known from Ardleigh, Asheldham, Epping, South Hanningfield, Nazeing, Ongar, Shoebury, Great Wakering and Walthamstow.

8. Jope *1961.*

9. Cunliffe *1968a.*

10. Allen *1961.* See also Hawkes *1968,* and Birchall *1965* for a discussion of the Continental origins of the *Belgae.*

11. Caesar *De Bello Gallico* v, 20-2.

12. Birchall *1965.*

13. Stead *1967.*

14. Peacock *in* Jesson and Hill *1971,* 161-88.

15. I am grateful to Miss V. Rigby for information on the Gallo-Belgic ware from Sheepen and Braughing. For a note by Allen on the coins from Braughing, see Stead *1970,* 45. A few sites in south Essex, notably Shoebury, have also produced Belgic pottery that appears to date from the first century B.C. (Birchall *1965*), and Mr. Drury tells me that pottery from Little Waltham shows Belgic influences in the first century B.C.

16. For a useful corpus of Belgic pottery from cemeteries, see Birchall *1965.*

17. Owles and Smedley *1967* (Boxford cemeteries).

18. These cemeteries are comparable in size to Swarling (17 graves) but much smaller than the King Harry Lane cemetery at Verulamium; Stead *1969.*

19. Frere *1967,* 41-2; Stevens, in Grimes *1951.*

20. Hawkes and Hull *1947,* 4-5. The Sheepen Cauldron must date from the late Bronze Age/early Iron Age transition.

21. Laver *1927.*

22. I am grateful to Mr. Crummy for information on Pitchbury.

23. For a summary of the 1970 excavations, *Britannia* ii (1971), 272. For the kilns, Hull *1963b.* For the 1930s excavations, Hawkes and Hull *1947.*

24. Birchall *1965,* 343 and *CMR* 1963-4. For earlier finds, May *1930* and Hawkes and Hull *1947,* 5.

25. It has been suggested that this bust came from a Belgic grave, on the grounds that only a contemporary would treasure the bust of this eccentric ruler. Caligula however was popular with the army, and this particular item could have come to Colchester in the baggage of a soldier during the Roman invasion three years after Caligula's death.

26. Allen *1967;* also a note by Allen, in Conlon *1973,* 41-6. Ptolemy lists *Salinae,* a name suggesting salt working, as lying in the Catuvellaunian territory. It is possible that south Essex, with its numerous red hills, did indeed lie in Catuvellaunian territory as

suggested by Rivet (1958). On the other hand the Catuvellaunian territory may have spread north-east to the Wash and *Salinae* may have lain here.

27. Allen *1970* and Frere *1941*.
28. Fox *1973*.
29. Owles *1969* and Brailsford *1972*.

2. HISTORY: A.D. 43-367

1. Dio 60.20; Suetonius, *Claudius* 17. See also Dudley and Webster *1965*.
2. Dio 62.21.5; Birley *1953*, 7.
3. I am grateful to Professor Hawkes for information on his work on the dykes. For Richborough, Cunliffe *1968b*, 232 and Bushe-Fox *1949*, 8-11.
4. Tacitus, *Annals* xii, 32. Two other military tombstones exist in the Colchester and Essex Museum; that of Facilis, centurion of the Twentieth legion, and that of another soldier, also possibly a centurion, who served in both the Second and Twentieth legions. Neither of these however is *definitely* a memorial to a *serving* soldier; they could be those of veterans from the *colonia*. The Facilis tombstone, however, seems to be pre-Boudiccan in date.
5. I am grateful to Mr. Crummy for information on his work in advance of full publication. For a brief note, Crummy *1973*. Generally pre-Flavian legionary fortresses in Britain seem to have been somewhat smaller than 50 acres (20 ha.).
6. For military finds, Dunnett *1971b*, 8-10 and 69, and Dunnett *1967*, 20.
7. *Britannia* iii (1972), 333.
8. Hull *1963a*, 63, fig. 15; Drury *1972*, 4-5; *1974*; *Britannia* iv (1973), 301.
9. For Orsett, *Trans. Essex Archaeol. Soc.* xi, pt 3 (3rd series), 338. For Tilbury, *Britannia* i (1970), 290-1. Mr. Rodwell has suggested that Tilbury may have marked a crossing point of the Thames, especially in view of the conquest period military occupation in the area, Rodwell *1972c*, 5. Dio, however, tells us that the crossing took place at the point where the Thames 'emptied into the sea', and although changes in the sea-level since Roman times in this part of Essex may mean that the present day tidal limit is different from the Roman one, a point upstream from Tilbury is indicated. A point near London Bridge is generally taken to be the spot, and the recent discovery of early military remains near Aldgate has lent support to this.
10. Hull *1963a*, 135.
11. For Wickford, *Britannia* iii (1972), 335. I am grateful to Mrs. Jones for information on Mucking.
12. I am grateful to Mr. Drury for information on his excavations at

Dunmow and Braintree in advance of publication.

13. Clarke *1952*, 151.
14. Rodwell *1972d*.
15. Webster, 'Fort. and town in early Roman Britain', in Wacher *1966*.
16. Rodwell *1972c*, 6.
17. Scattered finds of Belgic pottery in Silurian territory in South Wales probably reflect Belgic refugees there.
18. *Britannia* ii (1971), 272.
19. Tacitus, *Annals* xii, 32.
20. Tacitus, *Annals* xiv, 32.
21. Frere *1967*, 48. Allen *1970*, 15. For a concentration of torcs in north-west Norfolk, Owles *1969*.
22. Allen *1970*, 1-33.
23. It may be that in Roman eyes the mouth of the Thames estuary covered the entire coast from Richborough to Colchester. This would explain the curious reference in Tacitus (*Annals*, xiv, 32) to the spectacle of a phantom *colonia* overturned in the Thames, which he reports was seen at Colchester.
24. Richmond *1947*, 16.
25. Fishwick *1972*.
26. *Antiq. J.* xxxix (1959), 3.
27. For a detailed account of the rising, Dudley and Webster *1962*.
28. Tacitus *Annals*, xiv, 32.
29. The figures quoted by Tacitus should probably be taken with a pinch of salt.
30. Painter *1967*.
31. Webster *1970*, 193. For Chelmsford, *Britannia* iv (1973), 302, and Drury *1974*.
32. Mr. Rodwell first drew attention to this widespread burning. See for Chelmsford, Drury *1972*, 29, Drury *1974*; for Kelvedon, *Britannia* iii (1972), 286; for Rivenhall, Rodwell *1973*, 123.
33. Cunliffe *1968b*, 260-5 for a summary of the development of the Saxon Shore defences. For Dover, *Britannia* ii (1971), 286.
34. See also Hull *1963a*, 52-5.
35. *VCH Suffolk* i, 287-91.
36. *Britannia* iii (1972), 356.
37. Defoe *1722*.

3. COMMUNICATIONS AND URBAN SETTLEMENT

1. Margary *1957* and the Ordnance Survey Map of Roman Britain. For a detailed description of roads in Essex, Hull *1963a*, and for roads in Suffolk, Moore *1949*. For a recent discussion of the Antonine Itinerary, Rivet *1970*, especially 47, 52-3.
2. For Durolitum, Drury *1972*, 8; *Britannia* ii (1971), 274.
3. For Old Ford, Defoe *1722*; *Britannia* ii, 274.
4. Just outside Colchester the main London road was found to overlie a coin of Vespasian and later first century samian. *J. Brit.*

Archaeol. Ass. vii (3rd series) (1942), 53-70.

5. Long Melford, *Britannia* ii (1971), 271. Great Chesterford to Radwinter, Hull *1963a*, 28.
6. Hull *1963a*, 25.
7. Rodwell *1972c*, 11-13. For Billericay, *Britannia* iii (1972), 331.
8. Frere 1971.
9. Rivenhall, for instance, lies off the main London to Colchester road and is probably the centre of a large rural estate. Remains cover a wide area and include an apsidal building which in the past has been postulated as a *basilica.* It is just conceivable that Rivenhall rather than Kelvedon is the site of *Canonium.* Recently the existence of a small town has been suggested at Harlow, adjacent to the temple site (Conlon *1973*).
10. Tacitus, *Annals* xii, 32.
11. Wheeler *1919* and *1920*; Hull *1958*, 160-91.
12. Fishwick *1972*.
13. Hebditch *1971*.
14. Hebditch *1971*, 117; Hull *1960*; Dunnett *1971b*, 98.
15. Tacitus, *Annals* xiv, 32.
16. Dunnett *1968*; see also *Britannia* iii (1972), 331, modifying the views set out by the writer in 1968. More recent work has suggested that there was a whole suite of public buildings outside the original fortress.
17. I am grateful to Mr. Crummy for this information.
18. For a brief note, Crummy *1973*, *Britannia* iii (1972), 331.
19. Dunnett *1971b*, 29.
20. Dunnett *1967*.
21. For example in *insula* 39 in the later first century. Hull *1958*, 215-16, no. 105.
22. It is now clear that Colchester was supplied with piped water from the area west of the town. Since this was written, remains of what appears to have been a timber water tower have been found by Mr. Crummy outside the Balkerne Gate. This suggests that water was brought to the town under pressure. Mr. Crummy has also found traces of four timber water pipes taking water through the Gate and into the town, although the pipes were of a different date to that of the tower. *Current Archaeology* xliii (1974), 241.
23. Crummy *1973*.
24. Hull *1958*, 169-76; Hebditch *1971*, 117-18.
25. Dunnett *1971b*, 98; Crummy *1971*.
26. Dunnett *1971b*, 38, 85 (*insulae* 20 and 31) and Dunnett *1967*, 39-40 (*insula* 18).
27. As for instance was the massive wall in the centre of the *insula* 10 house (phase 7), Dunnett *1967*, 36-8.
28. Dunnett *1971b*, 44. I am grateful to Mr. Crummy for information on his recent work on the defences.
29. Dunnett *1971b*, 68-9.
30. For a convenient summary of the gate, Hull *1958*, 16-21. Recent

examination by Mr. Crummy suggests that the first 'destruction' of the gate, recorded by Wheeler, after which the north carriage-way was reduced in width and the central pier rebuilt in tufa, may instead have been simply the addition of flanking pedestrian ways and guard chambers to a pre-existing free standing gateway or triumphal arch. This perhaps stood in the line of the later first century earthwork defence, and marked the boundaries of the *colonia*, in a similar manner to the two triumphal arches at Verulamium which stood on the boundaries of the first century *municipium*.

31. Dunnett *1971b*, 52-3. For post-Boudiccan burnt levels elsewhere in the town, Hull *1958*, 213-14, 146; Dunnett *1971b*, 98-100; Crummy *1971*, 107-8.
32. Hebditch *1971*, 118-20. Excavations by the writer on the west side of the court are unpublished.
33. I am grateful to Mr. Crummy for this information in advance of publication.
34. For *insula* 10, Dunnett *1967*, 57; for *insula* 11, Dunnett *1971b*, 24-5. I am grateful to Mr. B.P. Blake for information on finds in *insula* 2.
35. The numbering adopted for the temples (see fig. 33) is that used in Lewis *1965*.
36. For extra-mural remains as a whole, Hull *1958*, 223-75.
37. For a summary of remains at Chelmsford known up until 1962, Brinson *in* Hull *1963a*, 63-71. For results of recent excavations, Drury *1972*, *1974*; *Britannia* iv (1973), 301-2. I am grateful to Mr. Drury for supplying information on his work in the town.
38. Rivet *1970*.
39. Stevens *1937*.
40. Drury *1972*, 13-28.
41. Todd *1970*.
42. For a summary of knowledge of the site until 1962, Brinson in Hull *1963a*, 72-88.
43. Rodwell *1972d*.
44. Brinson *in* Hull *1963a*, 82.
45. Information kindly supplied by Mr. Drury.
46. *Britannia* ii (1971), 273; iii (1972), 333. For Coddenham, *Antiq. J.* xxxvi (1956), 73-75.
47. *J. Roman Stud.* xliv (1959), 124. Information on Great Dunmow from Mr. Drury, and *Britannia* iv (1973), 304.
48. Hull *1963a*, 150. *J. Roman Stud.* xliii (1953), 150; *Britannia* iii (1972), 331; iv (1973), 305.
49. For the villa at Capel St. Mary, *Proc. Suffolk Inst. Archaeol.* xxv (1950), 209. For Stratford St. Mary, Colchester Museum Records.
50. Tacitus, *Annals* xiv, 32. See also Reynolds *in* Wacher *1966*.
51. Todd *1970*, 126.

4. RURAL SETTLEMENT

1. For a definition of the term 'villa', Rivet *1969*, 177.
2. Hull *1963a*, 158-9.
3. Hull *1963a*, 176.
4. Hull *1963a*, 192 (Tollesbury), 192 (Tolleshunt Knights), 176 (Salcott), 162 (Messing).
5. Hull *1963a*, 57-8, and observations by the writer in 1969.
6. For the original report on the site see *Trans. Essex Archaeol. Soc.* iii (1899), 136. For a summary, Hull *1963a*, 37-8. For the flue tiles, Lowther *1948*.
7. Hull *1963a*, 130-132.
8. Colchester Museum.
9. Hull *1963a*, 123 (Copford), 182 (Stanway).
10. Excavated by the Archaeological Research Group, Colchester. I am indebted to Mr. J. Blyth for information on his excavations here. See *J. Roman Stud.* lviii (1968), 197; lvii (1967), 189.
11. Hull *1963a*, 122 (Colne Engaine), 150 (Coggeshall Hall, Kelvedon).
12. Hull *1963a*, 137 and observation by Mr. J. Smallwood during fieldwork in 1967.
13. Hull *1963a*, 170-171.
14. For most of these sites see the relevant sections in Hull *1963a.* For Wickford, Rodwell *1971* and *1972a*, and for Ingatestone and Pleshey, notes made by Mr. Rodwell on his fieldwork in the Colchester Museum. I am grateful to Mr. Robertson of the Passmore Edwards Museum, Newham, for information on the sites at Abridge and Hornchurch and to Mrs. M.U. Jones for information from Mucking which suggests a nearby villa.
15. Hull *1963a*, 163-4. For a discussion of the relationship between villas and small towns, Todd *1970*, 124-8.
16. Hull *1963 a*, 17-20.
17. For a convenient summary of the nineteenth-century excavations, Hull *1963a*, 39-43.
18. *VCH Suffolk* i, 316; *Proc. Suffolk Inst. Archaeol.* iv (1929), 256.
19. Hull *1963a*, 159-60.
20. I am grateful to Mr. Crummy for information on this burial.
21. Brinson, in Hull *1963a*, 171-174. For summaries of his recent excavations, Rodwell *1972a*, *1972b* and *1973*.
22. Todd *1970*, 117.
23. I am grateful to the farmer, Mr. Cooper, for information on the site. For a note on bronze working, *Britannia* i (1970), 266-7.
24. Hull *1963a*, 183. A number of villas in the canton occur in pairs, e.g. Stebbing, Rivenhall, Stonham Aspel and Bartlow. The significance of this is not known.
25. For the pavement at Chadwell St. Mary with the results of excavations there, Manning *1962*. For that at East Tilbury, Hull *1963a*, 190. There are two areas at East Tilbury where extensive areas of occupation have been recorded, one at TQ 671756 (Hull

1963a, 190) and the other recently examined by Grays Thurrock Museum at TQ 690771.

26. Mucking. Information from the excavator Mrs. M.U. Jones; also *Britannia* iii (1972), 334. Information on North Shoebury from Mr. Macleod of Prittlewell Priory Museum, Southend-on-Sea. For Wendon's Ambo, *Britannia* iii (1972), 335. Information on Little Waltham from Mr. Drury.

27. See Richmond *1947*, 61, for his interpretation of the relevant passage in Tacitus, *Annals* xiv.

28. Bradford *1957*, Dilke *1971*.

29. Over the empire schemes of centuriation varied considerably, particularly in respect of the size of the *centuriae*. The normal measurement for a *centuria* seems to have been 20 x 20 *actus*, or a square measuring approximately 710 x 710 m., and covering 200 *iugera*. This measurement was not invariable and *centuriae* of 21 x 21, 20 x 24 and 20 x 16 *actus* are known. Three *centuriae* of normal dimensions would demand that the roads were 2,130 m. apart.

30. Haverfield *1918, 1920*. For a criticism of the argument, Richmond *1947* and Richmond *in* Hull *1963a*, 16. The apparently rectilinear layout of lanes in the Dengie peninsula reflects relatively modern land drainage schemes, not Roman centuriation as has been suggested.

31. Livy records grants made in 181 B.C. at Aquileia, where *pedites* received 50 *iugera* and centurions 100. At Florence all colonists received 50, but at Pisa perhaps only 30 (Bradford *1957*). Dilke (*1971*) records grants varying from 5 to 200 *iugera* per colonist.

32. Hull *1958*, 264 and pl. xl. For the Gosbecks site as a whole, 259-71.

33. Dunnett *1971a.*

34. For instance at Sanxay, Drevant and Vieux in Gaul.

35. For possible examples in south Scotland, Richmond *1955*, 136-7; and Woodeaton in Oxfordshire may turn out to have been another rural fairground.

36. For Harlow see the summary by France and Gobel *1968* and Davison *1973*.

5. INDUSTRY AND THE ECONOMY

1. Strabo iv 199; see also the iron shackles from Sheepen in connection with the pre-Roman slave trade.

2. For instance the storehouse in *insula* 10 at Colchester. It is also significant that in 54 B.C. Caesar apparently found the Trinovantes able to provide a large amount of corn for his army.

3. Brinson in Hull *1963a*, 84, and Manning *1972*.

4. *Britannia* i (1970), 292.

5. Hull *1963a*, 134.
6. Frere *1967*, 275.
7. See particularly note by Manning in *Antiquity* xl (1966), 60.
8. See *VCH Essex* i, 368-9.
9. Defoe *1722*.
10. *Britannia* iii (1972), 334.
11. For pearls, Tacitus, *Agricola* xii and Ammianus Marcellinus, *xxiii*, 6, 88. For oysters, Pliny, *Natural History* ix, 169, and xxxiii, 62; and Juvenal iv, 141.
12. I am grateful to Mr. Hull, and in particular to Mr. J.J. Heath, for comments on shells from my excavations in Colchester.
13. I am grateful to Mr. Drury for information in advance of full publication.
14. See Rodwell *1972c* for a suggestion that imported samian may have been unloaded at Canvey Island. Mr. A.F.J. Brown has suggested to me that the dispatch of corn by sea may explain the presence of some of the coastal villas.
15. I am grateful to the director, Mrs. K. de Brisay, for her comments on the subject. For interim reports, de Brisay *1972*, *1973* and *1974*. See also Hull *1963a*. Mr. Rodwell is undertaking research on red hills, particularly those in south Essex (Rodwell *1968*). A C14 date of 180 B.C. ± 40 from charcoal in the Maldon red hill suggests the site was in use in the pre-Roman Iron Age.
16. Remains of early kilns may well be very slight. See for example those at Rushden, Northants; *Britannia* iii (1972), 325-6.
17. Hawkes and Hull *1947*, 106. Pottery, including buff-coloured bowls and jugs, was found in a nearby well during the 1970 excavations at Sheepen and added to the number of forms represented in the kiln. Some of the pottery fragments were wasters.
18. Dunnett *1967*, 32.
19. Hull *1963b* is a comprehensive account of the Colchester kilns including the samian kiln.
20. Hull *1963b*, 17-19, fig. 19, also 34-43.
21. Young in Detsicas *1973*, 105-15.
22. Information from the Passmore Edward Museum (Rettenden), Hull *1963a*, 178 (Shoebury), Hull *1963a*, 137 (Halstead). A second kiln was found at Halstead by Mr. J. Smallwood in 1967. For Grays, *Britannia* ii (1971), 272; Tilbury, *Britannia* i (1970), 290; Sible Hedingham, Hull *1963a*, 145; Chadwell St. Mary, Hull *1963a*, 63; Sicklesmere and Martlesham, Ipswich Museum records; Ardleigh, Hull *1963a*, 38-9. Information on Mucking from the excavator, Mrs. M.U. Jones.
23. Hull *1963a*, 47. For Rushden, *Britannia* iii (1972) 325-6.
24. Tile kiln at Bures, *Colchester Archaeol. Grp. Bull.* xv; Stanningfield, Elmswell and Trimley St. Mary (probable site), Ipswich Museum records; Hull *1963a*, 56-7 (Braxted); Hull *1963a*, 35 (Alphamstone); Hull *1963a*, 45 (Ashdon); Hull *1963a*, 188 (Theydon Garnon).

25. Wissington, *Proc. Suffolk Inst. Archaeol.* xxxii, pt. 2 (1968), 210.
Pettistree, *Proc. Suffolk Inst. Archaeol.* ix (1934), 345. Melton-
Ipswich Museum records.
26. Lowther *1948*.
27. Hull *1963a*, 63 (Chadwell St. Mary); Dunnett *1967*, 35
(Colchester); Colchester Royal Grammar School site, information
from Mr. P. Crittenden; Chelmsford, information from Mr. M.G.
Davies; Kelvedon, observation by the writer on the southern side of
the settlement in 1968; Heybridge, information from Mr. Drury.
28. In Wacher *1966*, 84.
29. By Mr. J.D. Blyth and the Archaeological Research Group,
Colchester.
30. Leather offcuts have been found at Wickford, *Britannia* ii (1971),
273.

6. THE LATE FOURTH AND FIFTH CENTURIES

1. *Trans. Essex Archaeol. Soc.* 3rd series, ii, pt.3 (1970), 330 (for
Wickford); *Proc. Suffolk Inst. Archaeol.* i (1925), 74; xxii (1947),
334; xxiv (1949), 167; xxv (1950), 213 (for Ixworth).
2. Frere *1967*, 357.
3. Hawkes and Dunning *1961*, 1-70.
4. Holbert *1967*.
5. Wire's diaries are now preserved in the Colchester and Essex
Museum. For relevant extracts, Hull *1958*, 356-7.
6. Holbert *1965*.
7. Brinson, in Hull *1963a*, 72-6 (defences), 80-2 (fourth-century
building).
8. *Laeti* were settled on land within the empire, which they held in
return for military service. *Foederati* were barbarians who had
already raided and settled on frontier districts, who were then
bound by treaty with Rome to defend their land from further
attack (Alcock *1971*, 286). Mrs. Jones has drawn attention to the
ad hoc nature of the settlement and posed the question whether
Mucking may not have been a temporary encampment, used to
accommodate successive bands of Saxon immigrants straight from
the Continent (Jones *1974*).
9. Excavations at Mucking are still in progress and I am grateful to
Mrs. Jones for information on the site in advance of full
publication. See annual interim reports on the site in *J. Thurrock
Local Hist. Soc.* ii ff.; Jones *1968, 1969, 1972* and *1974;* Jones,
Evison and Myres *1968*, and Evison *1968*. For the early Saxon site
at Linford Quarry, Mucking, Barton *1962*; this site is adjacent to
Mucking and doubtless formed part of the same settlement.
10. West *1969*.
11. I am grateful to the excavator, Mr. Drury, for information on the

site at Heybridge in advance of publication, and to Mr. Macleod of
the Prittlewell Priory Museum, Southend, for information on Great
Stambridge, Shoebury and Great Wakering. For Wickford and
Rawreth, Rodwell *1971*, 19, and for Rivenhall, Rodwell *1972a*,
1972b and *1974*. For Tilbury, Bingley *1973*, and for pottery from
Little Oakley, Feering, Mucking and Great Stambridge, Myres
1969, 88.

12. *Britannia* iii (1972), 333.
13. Evison *1968*.
14. Myres *1969*, 95-7. For Rivenhall, Rodwell *1972a*, *1972b* and *1974*.
15. Evison *1968*, 231-249.
16. For Dunmow, *Britannia* ii (1971), 272. For Chelmsford, Drury
    1972.
17. Dodgson *1966*, 13-15. But see also Gelling *1967* for a suggestion
    that Wickham Market, Wickham Hall, Wickham St. Paul's and
    Wickham Bishops, all in the northern half of the canton and all
    names derived from the Old English *Wicham*, may also reflect very
    early Germanic settlement.
18. *VCH Suffolk* i, 311; *J. Roman Stud.* xxx (1940), 171; *Proc.
    Suffolk Inst. Archaeol.* i (1925), 74; xxii (1947), 334; xxiv (1949),
    167; xxv (1950), 213.
19. Hull *1958*, 36-41.
20. Hull *1958*, 19.
21. I am grateful to the excavator, Mr. Crummy, for this information.
22. Stenton *1943*, 53.
23. But see remarks by Alcock, *1971*, 311-12, on the dangers of using
    this evidence.

Bibliography

Alcock, L. (1971) *Arthur's Britain.*

Allen, D.F. (1961) The origins of coinage in Britain, in Frere, S.S. (ed.), *Problems of the Iron Age in Southern Britain* (London).

Allen, D.F. (1967) Celtic coins from the Romano-British temple at Harlow. *Brit. Numis. J.* xxxvi, 1.

Allen, D.F. (1970) The coins of the Iceni. *Britannia* i, 1.

Barton, K.J. (1962) Settlements of the Iron Age and Pagan Saxon periods at Linford, Essex. *Trans. Essex Archaeol. Soc.* 3rd ser. i, pt. II, 57.

Bingley, R. (1973) A Saxon *Grubenhaus* at West Tilbury. *J. Thurrock Local Hist. Soc.* xvi, 39.

Birchall, A. (1965) The Aylesford-Swarling culture: the problem of the Belgae reconsidered. *Proc. Prehist. Soc.* xxxi, 241.

Birley, E. (1953) *Roman Britain and the Roman Army* (Kendal).

Bradford, J. (1957) *Ancient Landscapes* (London).

Brailsford, J. and Stapley, J.E. (1972) The Impswich torcs. *Proc. Prehist. Soc.* xxxviii, 219.

Bushe-Fox, J.P. (1925) *The Excavation of the late Celtic Urnfield at Swarling* (Oxford).

Bushe-Fox, J.P. (1949) *Fourth Report on the Excavation of the Roman Fort at Richborough, Kent* (Oxford).

Clarke, D.T.-D. (1966) *Camulodunum and the Temple of Claudius* (Colchester Museum).

Clarke, R.R. (1940) The Iron Age in Norfolk and Suffolk. *Archaeol. J.* xcvi, 52.

Clarke, R.R. (1952) Roman Norfolk since Haverfield. *Norfolk Archaeol* xxx.

Clarke, R.R. (1960) *East Anglia* (London).

Conlon, R.F.B. (1973) Holbrooks. An Iron Age and Romano-British Settlement. Part 1. *Essex J.* viii, no 2, 30-50.

Crummy, P. (1971) *Insula 30. Trans. Essex Archaeol. Soc.* 3rd Ser. iii pt 1, 107.

Crummy, P. (1973) Recent excavations in Colchester. A note in the *Colchester Archaeol. Grp. Bull.* xvi, 14.

Cunliffe, B.W. (1968a) Early pre-Roman Iron Age communities in eastern England. *Antiq. J.* xlviii, 174.

Cunliffe, B.W. (1968b) *Fifth Report on the Excavation of the Roman Fort at Richborough, Kent* (Oxford).

Davison, K. (1973) Ancient Harlow *Essex J.* viii, no 2, 26.

de Brisay, K. (1972) A preliminary report on the exploration of the Red Hill at Osea Road, Maldon. *Colchester Archaeol. Grp. Bull.* xv.

de Brisay, K. (1973) A further report on the excavation of the Red Hill at Osea Road, Maldon. *Colchester Archaeol. Grp. Bull.* xvi, 20.

de Brisay, K. (1974) The excavation of a Red Hill at Peldon, Essex. Report on the first year. *Colchester Archaeol. Grp. Bull.* xvii.

Defoe, D. (1722) *A Tour Through the Eastern Counties.*

Detsicas, A. (ed.) (1973) *Current Research in Romano-British Coarse Pottery.* Council for British Archaeology Research Report 10.

Dilke, O.A.W. (1971) *The Roman Land Surveyors: An Introduction to the Agrimensores* (Newton Abbott).

Dodgson, J.M. (1966) The significance and distribution of the English place names in *ingas, inga,* in south-east England. *Mediaeval Archaeol.* x, 1.

Drury, P.J. (1972) Preliminary report, the Romano-British settlement at Chelmsford, Essex: Caesaromagos. *Trans. Essex Archaeol. Soc.* 3rd series, iv, 3.

Drury, P.J. (1973) Little Waltham. *Current Archaeol.* xxxvi, 10.

Drury, P.J. (1974) Chelmsford. *Current Archaeol.* xli, 166.

Dudley, D.R. and Webster, G. (1962) *The Revolt of Boudicca* (London).

Dudley, D.R. and Webster, G. (1965) *The Roman Conquest of Britain* (London)

Dunnett, B.R.K. (1967) Excavations on North Hill, Colchester, 1965. *Archaeol. J.* cxxxiii, 27.

Dunnett, B.R.K. (1968) First-century Colchester in the light of recent research. *Trans. Essex Archaeol. Soc.* 3rd ser. ii, pt. 2, 137.

Dunnett, B.R.K. (1971a) The excavation of the Roman theatre at Gosbecks. *Britannia* ii, 27.

Dunnett, B.R.K. (1971b) Excavations in Colchester 1964-8. *Trans. Essex Archaeol. Soc.* 3rd ser. iii, pt. 1, 1.

Dunnett, B.R.K. (1971c) Colchester. *Current Archaeol.* xxvi, 62.

Erith, F.H. and Holbert, P.R. (1970) The Iron Age A farmstead at Ardleigh, Colchester. *Colchester Archaeol. Grp. Bull.* xiii, pt. 4, 1.

Evans, A.J. (1890) On a late Celtic urn field at Aylesford, Kent, and on the Gaulish, Illyro-Italic and Classical connections of the forms of pottery and bronze work there discovered. *Archaeologia* lii, 388.

Evison, V. (1968) Quoit brooch style buckles. *Antiq. J.* xlviii pt. 2, 231.

Fishwick, D. (1972) Templum Divo Claudio Constitutum. *Britannia* iii (1972), 165.

Fox, A. and Pollard, S. (1973) A decorated bronze mirror from an Iron

Age settlement at Holcombe, near Uplyme, Devon. *Antiq. J.* liii, pt. 1, 16.

Fox, C. (1926) *The Archaeology of the Cambridge Region.* (Cambridge).

France, N.E. and Gobel, B.M. (1968) Harlow. *Current Archaeol.* xi, 287.

Frere, S.S. (1941) A Claudian Site at Needham, Norfolk. *Antiq. J.* xxi, 40.

Frere, S.S. (1967) *Britannia* (London).

Frere, S.S. (1971) The forum and baths at Caistor by Norwich. *Britannia* ii, 1.

Frere, S.S. (1972) *Verulamium* (London).

Gelling, M. (1967) English place names derived from the compound *wicham. Mediaeval Archaeol.* xi, 87.

Grimes, W.F. (ed.) (1951) *Aspects of Archaeology in Britain and beyond* (London).

Haverfield, F. (1918) Centuriation in Roman Britain. *English Hist. Rev.* xxxiii, 289.

Haverfield, F. (1920) Centuriation in Roman Essex. *Trans. Essex Archaeol. Soc.* 2nd ser. xv, 115.

Hawkes, C.F.C. (1968) New thoughts on the Belgae. *Antiquity* xliii, 6.

Hawkes, S. and Dunning, G.C. (1961) Soldiers and settlers in Britain; fourth to fifth century. *Mediaeval Archaeol.* v, 1.

Hawkes, C.F.C. and Hull, M.R. (1947) *Camulodunum* (London).

Hebditch, M. (1971) Excavations on the south side of the Temple Precinct at Colchester. *Trans. Essex Archaeol. Soc.* 3rd ser. iii, pt. 1, 115.

Holbert, P.R. (1965) The excavation of a section across the town ditch, Colchester, and the re-discovery and excavation of bastion 3. *Colchester Archaeol. Grp. Bull.*, viii, pt. 4, 22.

Holbert, P.R. (1967) Report on the excavation of a Roman road in the garden of 26, Lexden Road, Colchester. *Colchester Archaeol. Grp. Bull.* x, pt. 2, 21.

Holbert, P.R. (1971) Excavation of Roman tile kilns at Moat Farm, Lexden, Colchester, 1969-70. *Colchester Archaeol. Grp. Bull.* xiv, 22.

Hull, M.R. (1958) *Roman Colchester* (Oxford).

Hull, M.R. (1960) The St. Nicholas Church Site, Colchester. *Trans. Essex Archaeol. Soc. 2nd ser.* xxv, pt. 2, 300.

Hull, M.R. (1963a) *VCH Essex* iii, *Roman Essex* (Oxford).

Hull, M.R. (1963b) *The Roman Potters' kilns at Colchester* (Oxford).

Jesson, M. and Hill, D. (eds.) (1971) *The Iron Age and its Hillforts* (Southampton).

Jones, M.U. (1969) Saxon pottery from a hut at Mucking, Essex. *Berichten van de Rijksdienst voor het Oudheidkundig Bodemonderzoek. Jaargang,* xix, 145.

Jones, M.U. (1972) The Mucking, Essex crop mark sites. *Essex J.* vii, pt. 3, 1.

Jones, M.U. and W.T. (1974) The Early Saxon landscape at Mucking, Essex. *Brit. Archaeol. Rep.* 6.

Jones, M.U., Evison, V.I. and Myres, J.N.L. (1968) Crop mark sites at Mucking, Essex. *Antiq. J.* xlviii, pt. 2, 210.

Jope, E.M. (1961) Daggers of the early Iron Age in Britain. *Proc. Prehist. Soc.* xxvii, 304.

Laver, P.G. (1927) The excavation of a tumulus at Lexden, Colchester. *Archaeologia* lxxvi, 241.

Lewis, M.J.T. (1965) *Temples in Roman Britain* (Cambridge).

Lowther, A.W.G. (1948) *A study of the patterns on Roman flue tiles and their distribution.* Surrey Archaeol. Soc. Res. Paper no. 1.

Manning, W.H. (1962) Excavation of an Iron Age and Roman site at Chadwell St. Mary. *Trans. Essex Archaeol. Soc.* 3rd ser., i, pt. 2, 127.

Manning, W.H. (1972) Ironwork hoards in Iron Age and Roman Britain. *Britannia* iii, 224.

Margary, I.D. (1957) *Roman Roads in Britain*, vol. 2 (London).

May, T. (1930) *Catalogue of Roman Pottery in the Colchester and Essex Museum* (Cambridge).

Moore, I.E. (1949) Roman Suffolk. *Proc. Suffolk Inst. Archaeol.* xxiv, 168.

Myres, J.N.L. (1969) *Anglo-Saxon Pottery and the Settlement of England* (Oxford).

Owles, E. (1969) The Ipswich gold torcs. *Antiquity* xliii, 171.

Owles, E. and Smedley, N. (1967) Two Belgic cemeteries at Boxford. *Proc. Suffolk Inst. Archaeol.* xxxi, pt. 1, 88.

Painter, K.S. (1967) A Roman bronze helmet from Hawkedon. *Proc. Suffolk Inst. Archaeol.* xxxi, pt. 1, 57.

Richmond, I.A. (1947) The four *coloniae* of Roman Britain. *Archaeol. J.* ciii, 57.

Richmond, I.A. (1955) *Roman Britain.* (London).

Rivet, A.L.F. (1958) *Town and Country in Roman Britain* (London).

Rivet, A.L.F. (ed.) (1969) *The Roman Villa in Britain.* (London).

Rivet, A.L.F. (1970) The British section of the Antonine Itinerary. *Britannia* i, 34.

Rodwell, W. (1968) The excavation of a Red Hill on Canvey Island. *Trans. Essex Archaeol. Soc.* 3rd ser. ii, pt. 2, 14.

Rodwell, W. (1970) Some Romano-Saxon pottery from Essex. *Antiq.' J.* l, 262.

Rodwell, W. (1971) *South-east Essex in the Roman Period* (Southend Museum).

Rodwell, W. (1972a) Rivenhall. *Current Archaeol.* xxx, 184.

Rodwell, W. (1972b) Rivenhall. *Colchester Archaeol. Grp. Bull.* xv.

Rodwell, W. (1972c) *Roman Essex* (Essex Archaeol. Soc.).

Rodwell, W. (1972d) A Roman fort at Great Chesterford, Essex. *Britannia* iii, 290.

Rodwell, W. and K. (1973) The Roman villa at Rivenhall, Essex: an interim report. *Britannia* iv, 115.

Smith, R.A. (1912) On late Celtic antiquities discovered at Welwyn, Herts. *Archaeologia* lxiii, 1.

Stead, I.M. (1967) A La Tène III burial at Welwyn Garden City. *Archaeologia* ci, 1.

Stead, I.M. (1969) Verulamium 1964-1968. *Antiquity* xliii, 45.

Stead, I.M. (1970) A trial excavation at Braughing, 1969. *Hertfordshire Archaeol.* ii, 37.

Stenton, F. (1943) *Anglo-Saxon England* (Oxford).

Stevens, C.E. (1937) Gildas and the *civitates* of Britain. *English Hist. Rev.* lii, 193.

Stevens, C.E. (1941) Gildas Sapiens. *English Hist. Rev.* lvi, 353.

Todd, M. (1970) The small towns of Roman Britain. *Britannia* i, 114.

Wacher, J.S. (ed.) (1966) *The Civitas Capitals of Roman Britain* (Leicester).

Webster, G. (1970) The military situation in Britain between A.D. 43 and 71. *Britannia* i, 179.

West, S.E. (1969) The Anglo-Saxon village of West Stow: an interim report on excavations 1965-8. *Mediaeval Archaeol.* xiii, 1.

Wheeler, R.E.M. (1920) A further note on the vaults under Colchester Castle. *J. Roman Stud.* x, 87.

Wheeler, R.E.M. (1928) A Romano-Celtic temple near Harlow, Essex, and a note on the type. *Antiq. J.* viii, 300.

Wheeler, R.E.M. (1929) Old England, Brentford. *Antiquity* iii, 20.

Wheeler, R.E.M. and Laver, P.G. (1919) Roman Colchester. *J. Roman Stud.* ix, 146.

Wooldridge, S.W. and Linton, D.L. (1933) The loam-terrains of south-east England and their relation to its early History. *Antiquity* vii, 297.

Index